Your Family Records

How to Preserve Personal, Financial & Legal History

By Carol Pladsen & Denis Clifford

Illustrated by Mari Stein

Please read this: We have done our best to give you useful and accurate information. But please be aware that laws and procedures are constantly changing and are subject to differing interpretations. You have the responsibility to check all material you read here before relying on it. Of necessity, neither Nolo Press nor the authors make any guarantees concerning the information in this book or the use to which it is put.

Book Design & Layout	*Toni Ihara*
Production	*Stephanie Harolde*
Illustrations	*Mari Stein*
Typesetting	*Image Factory*

Printing History

Nolo Press is committed to keeping its books up-to-date. Each new printing, whether or not it is called a new edition, has been completely revised to reflect the latest law changes. If you're using this book any considerable time after the last date listed below, be particularly careful not to rely on information without checking it.

First Edition	May 1984
Second Printing	September 1984
Second Edition	January 1987

ISBN 0-87337-036-8
Library of Congress Catalog Card No.: 84-60121

Acknowledgments

We would like to thank a number of people. Our family and friends for their helpful comments — Walter and Trudy Warner, Beatrice Pladsen, Paul and Catherine Clifford, Wendell and Patsy Jackson, Paul and Marjorie Reigstad, Abby Goldman, Trudy Ahlstrom, Amy Ihara, Yuri Moriwaki, Cathy Stevenson, Terri Hearsh and Anna Weidman. A special thanks to those people who contributed their significant editorial skills — Jake Warner (a one-of-a-kind editor), Brad Bunnin, Liz Ryan, Steve Elias and Susan Doran. Credit and our thanks for the design and production of the book go to Toni Ihara, Mari Stein, Stephanie Harolde, Glenn Voloshin and Keija Kimura. The book is now in the hands of the other competent people at Nolo Press — Charlotte Johnson and Kate Miller who see to it people know about the book, John O'Donnell and Jack Devaney who see to it people receive the book and Barbara Hodovan who keeps track of it all.

Table of Contents

Introduction

This book supplies you with the forms and instructions for organizing your legal, financial and personal records. Our central purpose is to give you one well organized place in which to record your important information. We have struggled mightily to make these materials both easy to use and comprehensive. In the process we have learned a lot about our own families, discovered forgotten personal and financial records and generally gotten to know ourselves better. We truly hope you have the same experience.

This book is designed to help you in three principal ways:

● First, we provide a detailed structure which will enable you to record all your basic financial, legal and practical information in one place. Our purpose here is not only to supply you with a good record keeping device, but to encourage you to carefully review your affairs. By the time you are done, you should have the peace of mind that comes with knowing that those who will handle your business and personal matters after your death will not have to sort through two shoe boxes, three desk drawers and mounds of paper.

• Second, the book is designed to assist you in preserving your personal and family history. You are a crucial link between generations. By recording the important facts and events of your life, as well as those of your parents and grandparents, you can build a bridge from the past to your children and grandchildren.

• Finally, we will give you a mild dose of estate planning information. Since the process of organizing your financial affairs inevitably raises questions of how best to pass property to family and friends this is an appropriate time to consider wills and other estate planning methods.

The financial and practical information to be recorded in Part I of the book must be focused and specific for maximum usefulness. The death of any family member is painful. You can do a real service to those who survive you by presenting them with an orderly, thoughtful record of the information necessary to manage your financial and personal matters efficiently. Anyone who has handled estate matters (as the authors have) can tell you what a dreadful task it can be if you can't find the insurance policy, don't know where bank accounts are, and are suddenly faced with notifying relatives no one has been in touch with for eons. So, if while compiling your financial data you encounter difficulty locating a particular piece of information, imagine how much more difficult it would be for your family or friends if you did not do a careful job.

Part II, for recording family history and memories, should be fun to prepare. You know all sorts of bits and pieces of unique information and have insights that your family will surely want to know too. Write them down. In our age of mobility, when extended families and the tradition of oral history are largely a thing of the past, you cannot depend on anyone else to preserve your knowledge for you. But then, perhaps you never could. Certainly the French scholar Beaumanoir didn't think so when he wrote in 1283, "... for the memory of men slips and flows away, and the life of man is short and that which is not written is soon forgotten."

A thorough organization of your financial affairs must inevitably include a bit of estate planning. In Part III, we provide an overview of estate planning for the modest to moderate sized estate. For our purposes, estate planning is best defined as preparing for the efficient transfer of your property at your death so that your inheritors receive as much of it as possible and lawyers and taxing authorities receive only the legal minimum. At Nolo Press we believe strongly in self-help law. Therefore, rather than simply urging you to turn your problems over to an attorney, we explain the basics of estate planning. Armed with this information, you can sensibly decide whether you want to do the work of planning your estate or whether you prefer outside help. If you're like a lot of people these days, you will probably choose a combination of both.

Part IV of the book is blank. This is your place to continue any of the material that doesn't fit in the spaces we supply in Parts I & II. Of necessity, we made arbitrary choices as to how much you might want to include under the various headings. From time to time, you will surely want to write at more length on an area of particular interest or to include material on a subject for which we haven't provided an entry.

Here are some suggestions on how best to use this book:

• Try to make the gathering of information a relaxed and enjoyable undertaking. Rushing is unlikely to be either productive or fun. Memories, in particular, cannot always be recalled on command, but often emerge from our minds at unexpected times.

• For lengthier writings of family history or personal memories, it's wise to do a draft or two on separate sheets of paper before entering anything here. Your writings are intended to last, so you want them to be as clear, accurate and to-the-point as possible. This will inevitably require some rewriting. This book, for example, has gone through at least seven drafts.

- ● Circulate copies of the appropriate pages of Part II to family members or friends who might have other interesting information, memories or comments to offer.

- ● As you complete and polish your information, you will want to record it in this book. Part II should be recorded in ink for permanence. However, the practical and financial information in Part I should be written in pencil so that you can make necessary changes over time.

- ● Review and update the book periodically. If you change information, date the second entry to avoid possible confusion about which information is most current.

- ● Make sure several people know of the book and its location.

- ● You may well prefer to keep some of the information listed here safe, secure and private. For example, you might not want to risk having the combination of your safe written in a book which is kept on an open bookshelf, or you may want to protect some particularly private aspect of your life (or someone else's) from inquiring eyes. For this reason, our publisher has perforated all the pages at the left hand margin for easy removal. Of course, the location of any material stored in a safe deposit box or other secure place should be indicated in the book.

- ● If you run out of space under any heading in Part I or Part II, continue the entry on one of the blank pages in Part IV. At the end of the entry to be continued, give the page number where the additional information is to be found. For example, if you run out of space in Part IIC and continue it on page 176, write "continued on page 176" at the bottom of your entry in Part IIC. Then, on the top of page 176, write "Part IIC continued."

Now, a few words for couples. When preparing our initial outline for this book, it gradually became clear to us that to provide a format suited to a couple would be impossibly cumbersome. There are so many areas where personal and family history and even financial situations can vary, that a single volume for a couple would be almost twice this size, as well as burdened with complicated instructions. The only truly negative aspect of this reality, we decided, was the expense of buying a second book, which can be a real burden for people on fixed incomes. When we shared our concerns with our publisher they came up with what we think is a fair solution. Nolo Press has included a coupon at the back of this book allowing you to buy one additional *Your Family Records* for less than half the retail price, or $5.95.

Finally, we would like to say that we see your family records as a gift from you to younger generations and as such your completed book becomes a creative work that appeals to the curious and loving parts of the human spirit. We hope your gift endures and brings deep satisfaction to you and your family.

Financial Data
and Personal Records

A. How to Get Started

The following pages in Part I are designed for you to list information regarding your practical affairs, including financial data and personal records which you want your family or other inheritors to know. As a matter of common sense, it is wise to consolidate this information. More importantly, doing so should simplify and speed the eventual transfer of assets to your inheritors. There is quite a lot of information to gather and record. Thoroughness is most important, so don't rush.

The major categories of information you will want to record are divided into sections identified by capital letters. (For example, this is Part I, Section A.) Many sections are divided into subsections that are identified by lower case letters. This format is designed to help you organize your information. It is also intended to provide a ready cross-reference to the appropriate sections of Part III entitled, "Transferring Your Property: Estate Planning." Remember, every bit of property you list in Part I will have to be transferred at your death unless you give it away or use it up first. For this reason, you may well want to think about your estate plan as you go along.

As we discussed in the introduction, if you need more space for any item, use the blank pages provided at the end of the book. To be sure a future reader can readily find "continued" material make a note, as part of the original entry, the specific page number where the continuation can be found.

If any information requested by the forms that follow is not relevant to you, leave the space blank or mark it "not applicable" or "n/a". Don't worry if you end up with plenty of blank spaces. Of necessity we have included blanks for all sorts of possible information. No one family will need it all. If we have not provided enough, or any space, for something important to you, retitle one of the unused spaces or record it at the back of the book in Part IV.

VALUABLE DOCUMENTS AND PRIVATE INFORMATION NOTE: You may want to keep some of your information private, such as the location of jewelry, cash, bank books or combinations to locks and safes. For this reason the pages have been perforated so they can be removed to protect confidential information. Any pages you remove should be kept in a secure place, such as a safe deposit box. If someone will need to obtain these pages quickly in order to handle your affairs, be sure to indicate in Part I, Section U where they are, and what arrangements you've made to provide prompt and suitable access to them.

LOCATION SYMBOLS: The symbol  is used throughout the book whenever the location of any object, document or other property is given. This will make it easy for the people who take care of your affairs to quickly focus on what tangible objects need to be collected and where they are located.

B. Ready Money

Nothing that is God's is obtainable by money
— Tertullian

This is where you list your bank accounts (checking and savings), credit union funds, certificates of deposit (C. D.'s), money market funds, traveller's checks, piggy banks and anything you may have under the mattress or buried in a can in the backyard. Bank cards, for use at an automatic teller, are listed here, while bank credit cards (Visa, MasterCard) are listed in Part I, Section I.

a. Financial Accounts — Demand Accounts

Include all your accounts for which there is little or no penalty for immediate withdrawal and short notice can be given to get your money. These normally include checking accounts, regular passbook savings, most credit union accounts, negotiable treasury bills, money market funds and money market instruments (negotiable certificates of deposit, commercial paper, bonds and bankers' acceptances). If you have accounts where money must be kept on deposit for a set term to qualify for significant interest or tax benefits, it is covered in the next section.

Financial institution's name _____

Address _____

_____

Your account number_____ Type of account_____

Person to contact_____ Phone_____
(banker, broker, etc.)

The account is: Individual ___ Joint tenancy ___ Tenants in common ___ Co-ownership ___

Under a trust provision ___ Other _____*

Additional details of ownership _____

_____

Location of your papers and records _____

⊗

Financial institution's name _____

Address _____

_____

Your account number_____ Type of account_____

Person to contact_____ Phone_____
(banker, broker, etc.)

The account is: Individual ___ Joint tenancy ___ Tenants in common ___ Co-ownership ___

Under a trust provision ___ Other _____

Additional details of ownership _____

_____

Location of your papers and records _____

*Many people hold accounts jointly or as co-owners or in trust for another. This is discussed in Part III, Step 9. If you are unsure about the meaning of these terms read this material.

Financial institution's name _____

Address_____

_____

Your account number_____ Type of account_____

Person to contact_____ Phone_____
(banker, broker, etc.)

The account is: Individual ___ Joint tenancy ___ Tenants in common ___ Co-ownership ___

Under a trust provision ___ Other _____

Additional details of ownership_____

_____

Location of your papers and records _____

Additional information _____

_____

_____

b. Financial Accounts—Term Accounts

   Here is where you should list accounts which have a penalty for early withdrawal such as certificates of deposit and other term accounts. We have placed IRAs and Keoghs in Section K under retirement benefits.
   NOTE: The penalty connected with these accounts is usually eliminated with the death or disability of the investor.

Financial institution's name _____

Address_____

_____

Your account number_____ Type of account_____

Person to contact_____ Phone_____
(banker, broker, etc.)

Length of term _____

Penalty for early withdrawal _____

The account is: Individual ___ Joint tenancy ___ Tenants in common ___ Co-ownership ___

Under a trust provision ___ Other _____

Additional details of ownership _____

_____

Location of your papers and records _____

——————————————⊗——————————————

Financial institution's name _____

Address _____

_____

Your account number_____ Type of account_____

Person to contact_____ Phone_____
(banker, broker, etc.)

Length of term _____

Penalty for early withdrawal _____

The account is: Individual ___ Joint tenancy ___ Tenants in common ___ Co-ownership ___

Under a trust provision ___ Other _____

Additional details of ownership _____

_____

Location of your papers and records _____

——————————————⊗——————————————

Financial institution's name _____

Address _____

Your account number_____ Type of account_____

Person to contact_____ Phone_____
(banker, broker, etc.)

Length of term _____

Penalty for early withdrawal _____

The account is: Individual ___ Joint tenancy ___ Tenants in common ___ Co-ownership ___

Under a trust provision ___ Other _____

Additional details of ownership_____

Location of your papers and records _____

Financial institution's name _____

Address_____

Your account number_____ Type of account_____

Person to contact_____ Phone_____
(banker, broker, etc.)

Length of term _____

Penalty for early withdrawal _____

The account is: Individual ___ Joint tenancy ___ Tenants in common ___ Co-ownership ___

Under a trust provision ___ Other _____

Additional details of ownership_____

Location of your papers and records _____

A feast is made for laughter,
and wine maketh merry:
But money answereth
all things.
— Ecclesiastes 10:19

c. Cash

How much _____

Location(s) _____

_____

People to contact (if any) _____

d. Other Ready Money
(traveller's checks, automatic teller bank card, cashier checks, gold, silver, other)

_____

_____

Location(s) _____

_____

People to contact or codes (if any) _____

Additional information _____

_____

C. Real Estate

List all your real property including the house, condominium, or co-op apartment where you live; rental property, your house in the country (if you're lucky enough to have one); improved real property, rental units, etc. If you own a mobile home, you should also list it here, whether or not you own the land it is on. Motor homes, car trailers, and other vehicles which routinely move along the highways should be listed in Section F, below.

a. Your Home

Address _____

_____

Date of purchase _____ Purchase price _____

Mortgage payments*

        1st Mortgage total $_____ $_____ per month

        Pay to _____   Date Due_____

        2nd Mortgage $_____ $_____ per month

        Pay to _____   Date Due_____

Property tax (yearly) $_____ $_____ Per (month, bi-annual)_____

  Method of payment: Included in mortgage____ Paid directly____

  If paid directly, to whom _____

_____

Other obligations against property such as tax _____
liens, loan security agreements, etc.

_____

Ownership is: Sole____ Joint tenancy____ Tenants-in-common ____ Held in trust ____ Other_____

Additional ownership information _____

Estimated present market value _____

  Your Equity_____ ** As of _____

Additional information _____

_____

*A mortgage can go by other names, such as "Deed of Trust."
**Your equity is the current market value less what you owe on the house and the cost of selling it.

Location of deed, mortgage papers, other documents such as homeowner insurance policy, repair documents, tax records, etc. _____

_____

b. Mobile Home

Address _____

_____

Date of purchase _____ Purchase price _____

Mortgage payments

1st Mortgage total $ _____ $ _____ per month

Pay to _____ Date Due _____

2nd Mortgage $ _____ $ _____ per month

Pay to _____ Date Due _____

Property tax (yearly) $ _____ $ _____ Per (month, bi-annual) _____

Method of payment: Included in mortgage _____ Paid directly _____

If paid directly, to whom _____

_____

Other obligations against property such as tax liens, loan security agreements, etc. _____

_____

Ownership is: Sole ___ Joint tenancy ___ Tenants-in-common ___ Held in trust ___ Other ___

Additional ownership information _____

Estimated present market value _____

Your Equity _____ As of _____

Additional information _____

_____

Manufacturer _____

Model _____ I.D. Number _____

Name of landowner _____ Phone _____
(if on leased, rented land)
Address _____

_____

Terms of your land or park lease _____

Location of ownership papers, deeds, _____
leases, insurance, repair documents _____

Mid pleasures and palaces though we may roam, be it
ever so humble, there's no place like home.
— J. H. Payne

c. Co-op/Condominium

Address _____

_____

Date of purchase _____ Purchase price _____

Mortgage payments

1st Mortgage total $ _____ $ _____ per month

Pay to _____   Date Due _____

2nd Mortgage $ _____ $ _____ per month

Pay to _____   Date Due _____

Property tax (yearly) $ _____ $ _____ Per (month, bi-annual) _____

Method of payment: Included in mortgage ____ Paid directly ____

If paid directly, to whom _____

_____

Other obligations against property such as tax _____
liens, loan security agreements, etc. _____

Ownership is: Sole ___ Joint tenancy ___ Tenants-in-common ___ Held in trust ___ Other _____

Additional ownership information _____

16

Estimated present market value _____

Your Equity _____ As of _____

Additional information _____

_____

Name of management organization _____

Address _____

_____

Person to contact _____ Phone _____

Name of project _____ Unit # _____

Address _____

_____

Membership dues _____ Terms _____

Additional information _____

_____

Location of ownership documents,
association agreements, insurance, repair   _____
documents, etc.   _____

d. Other Real Estate

Address _____

_____

Date of purchase _____ Purchase price _____

Mortgage payments

1st Mortgage total $ _____ $ _____ per month

Pay to _____   Date Due _____

2nd Mortgage $ _____ $ _____ per month

Pay to _____   Date Due _____

Property tax (yearly) $_____ $_____ Per (month, bi-annual)_____

    Method of payment: Included in mortgage_____ Paid directly_____

    If paid directly, to whom _____

Other obligations against property such as tax
liens, loan security agreements, etc.   _____

_____

_____

Ownership is: Sole____ Joint tenancy____ Tenants-in-common____ Held in trust____ Other_____

Additional ownership information _____

Estimated present market value_____

    Your Equity_____   As of _____

Additional information _____

_____

Type_____
      (house, apartment, undeveloped land, etc.)

People to contact (manager, tenant, handyman,   _____ Phone_____
real estate agent)   _____ Phone_____

    _____ Phone_____

Location of ownership papers, deeds,
leases, insurance, repair documents   _____

_____

"Buy Land. They aren't making any more of it."
— Mark Twain

Address_____

_____

Date of purchase_____ Purchase price_____

Mortgage payments

1st Mortgage total $_____ $_____ per month

Pay to_____ Date Due_____

2nd Mortgage $_____ $_____ per month

Pay to_____ Date Due_____

Property tax (yearly) $_____ $_____ Per (month, bi-annual)_____

Method of payment: Included in mortgage_____ Paid directly_____

If paid directly, to whom _____

_____

Other obligations against property such as tax _____
liens, loan security agreements, etc.

_____

Ownership is: Sole___ Joint tenancy___ Tenants-in-common___ Held in trust___ Other_____

Additional ownership information _____

Estimated present market value_____

Your Equity_____ As of _____

Additional information _____

_____

Type_____
        (house, apartment, undeveloped land, etc.)

_____ Phone_____

People to contact (manager, tenant, handyman,
real estate agent)   _____ Phone_____

_____ Phone_____

D. Financial Advisors and Securities
(stocks, bonds, etc.)

We use the word "security" to mean your ownership or property interest in a business or enterprise run by others. Stock is the most common, and best known, type of security, but the term is much broader. Your mutual fund shares are also securities, as are any commodities futures, private or government bonds, stock options, or limited partnership interests you are fortunate enough to own. There are, of course, many other types of securities, some fairly esoteric. Suffice it to say that if you own passive shares in some- one else's profit-making enterprise, this information should be listed here. This is not the place to list money owed you on essentially personal loans, however, even if they are secured by a mortgage or some other security. We cover personal debts in Section H.

We have divided this section into two general areas. The first is for your financial advisors and/or brokers; the second is where you should list your securities themselves. If you are an active trader, or have numerous securities, it may not be practical to list every investment. As an alternative you may simply want to record your active broker- age accounts or the location of your files, securities ledger or other record keep- ing devices.

VARIOUS SECURITIES

a. Stockbrokers

Stockbroker's name _____ Phone _____

Broker's company _____

Address _____

_____

Your account number _____

Other information _____

Stockbroker's name _____ Phone _____

Broker's company _____

Address _____

_____

Your account number _____

Other information _____

b. Other Investment Advisors or Brokers Who Should Be Contacted

Name _____ Phone _____

Company _____

Address _____

_____

Other information _____

Name _____ Phone _____

Company _____

Address _____

_____

Other information _____

c. Your Stock

List whether your stock is common, preferred or whether you have stock options, etc. If you are involved in complicated matters such as selling stock short, standing buy or sell orders or margin accounts include details under "Additional information."

Company	Type	Number of Shares	Purchase Price	Date of Purchase	Location of Certificates	Exchanged/ Traded On

Company	Type	Number of Shares	Purchase Price	Date of Purchase	Location of Certificates	Exchanged/ Traded On

Stock Value _____ as of _____

d. Your Mutual Funds

Company	Name	Address	Number of shares	Purchase price	Date of purchase

Mutual funds value _____ as of _____

e. Other Securities

This should include commodity futures, corporate, municipal or federal bonds, gold or silver certificates.

Company	Type	Number of Shares	Purchase Price	Date of Purchase	Location of Certificates	Exchanged/ Traded On

Value of other securities _____ as of _____

Net value of stock, mutual funds and other securities _____

Additional information about stocks, mutual funds, other securities

_____

_____

E. Business Ownership/Other Investments

In this land of free enterprise, a privately held business can be the bulk of a person's wealth. If you own a business or a part of one list the main facts about it in the space below. Then summarize in narrative form other essential information. Please understand, however, that this section is not designed for recording extensive information regarding substantial business ownership or properties, since these matters are almost always far too complicated for a short list. At any rate it is not necessary to record such information here as all businesses keep extensive financial and management information as part of their regular records. The purpose of this book is to provide an overview of your business interests and to indicate where your detailed business information and records can be found.

NOTE: This section is different from Part I, Section D (Securities and Financial Advisors). Here you list your investments in those businesses in which you have a say in management. In other words, if you own 100 shares in General Motors, you list them in Section D, but if you own 100 shares in Sam's Drug Store (and you're Sam), list your investment here.

a. Your Business

Name of Business _____

Address _____

_____

Type of business organization (sole proprietor,
partnership, corporation, etc.) _____

If a partnership, percentage you own _____

Name of other partner(s) _____

_____

Address(es) _____

_____

If a corporation, number of shares you own _____ Total shares issued _____

Names of other principal shareholders _____

_____

Addresses_____

_____

Money you owe business (if any)_____

Location of business papers
and financial records_____

_____

Key people with essential information (people in charge, managers, lawyers, accountants)

Name	Position	Address	Phone

Net value of your business interests $_____ as of _____

Additional information_____

_____

_____

_____⊗_____

Name of Business_____

Address_____

_____

Type of business organization (sole proprietor,
partnership, corporation, etc.)_____

If a partnership, percentage you own_____

Name of other partner(s)_____

_____

Address(es)_____

_____

If a corporation, number of shares you own _____ Total shares issued _____

Names of other principal shareholders_____

_____

Addresses_____

_____

Money you owe business (if any)_____

Location of business papers
and financial records_____

_____

Key people with essential information (people in charge, managers, lawyers, accountants)

Name	Position	Address	Phone

Net value of your business interests $_____ as of _____

Additional information_____

_____

_____

b. Other investments/ownerships.

Include any partnership share or corporate share interests not already listed. If you
have any interest in oil wells, land trusts or other investments list them here as well.

Type of asset_____

Name and specific description_____

Address/Location_____

_____

People to contact (name/address/phone) _____

_____

Purchase price or terms of acquisition _____

Date of purchase _____

Estimated present value _____ as of _____

Other owners _____

Additional information _____

LOCATION   Location of ownership
papers or documents _____

———————————————⊗———————————————

Type of asset _____

Name and specific description _____

Address/Location _____

_____

People to contact (name/address/phone) _____

_____

Purchase price or terms of acquisition _____

Date of purchase _____

Estimated present value _____ as of _____

Other owners _____

Additional information _____

LOCATION   Location of ownership
papers or documents _____

———————————————⊗———————————————

Type of asset _____

Name and specific description _____

Address/Location _____

_____

People to contact (name/address/phone) _____

_____

Purchase price or terms of acquisition _____

Date of purchase _____

Estimated present value _____ as of _____

Other owners _____

Additional information _____

Location of ownership
papers or documents _____

───────────────── ⊗ ─────────────────

Type of asset _____

Name and specific description _____

Address/Location _____

_____

People to contact (name/address/phone) _____

_____

Purchase price or terms of acquisition _____

Date of purchase _____

Estimated present value _____ as of _____

Other owners _____

Additional information _____

Location of ownership
papers or documents _____

Money is a good servant, but a bad master.
— Old Proverb

c. Intellectual Property

If you have any copyrights, patents, trademarks, film residuals or other intellectual property you should record significant information concerning it here.

Type of property _____

Name of company holding rights under your license
(publisher, manufacturer, etc.)

_____

Address _____

_____

Person to contact _____ Phone _____

Basis of your ownership right _____ _____

_____

Location of contracts or other documents _____

_____

State and/or federal registration (i.e. copyright, _____
patent, trademark)

_____

Registration office _____ Registration date _____

Registration number _____

Location of documents _____

Other owners _____

⬥

Type of property _____

Name of company holding rights under your license
(publisher, manufacturer, etc.)

_____

Address _____

_____

Person to contact _____ Phone _____

Basis of your ownership right _____

_____

Location of contracts or other documents _____

_____

State and/or federal registration (i.e. copyright, _____
patent, trademark)

_____

Registration office _____ Registration date _____

Registration number _____

Location of documents _____

Other owners _____

—————————————⊗—————————————

Type of property _____

Name of company holding rights under your license
(publisher, manufacturer, etc.)

_____

Address _____

_____

Person to contact _____ Phone _____

Basis of your ownership right _____

_____

Location of contracts or other documents _____

_____

State and/or federal registration (i.e. copyright, _____
patent, trademark) _____

Registration office_____ Registration date_____

Registration number_____

 Location of documents_____

Other owners_____

F. Vehicles

Here you should list your automobiles, motorcycles, trucks, vans, boats, snowmobiles, trains, jets, etc. Include recreational vehicles, trailers and other "live-in" vehicles which can be licensed to go on the highways. Mobile homes, however, should be listed in Part I, Section B (Real Estate). The information you will want to provide will vary depending on the type of vehicle. In some cases, for example, location of the vehicle is important, such as where a boat is docked, and the substance of any docking agreement. Financial information concerning payments, liens, etc. is also important. Repair information such as the names and addresses of mechanics, maintenance hints, or special problems can also be helpful. In this regard, there is space for more detailed repair instructions in Section R. Vehicle insurance is covered in Section J.

Make, model, serial # _____

Purchase price _____ Date purchased _____

Purchased from _____

License # and state _____

Co-owner _____

Does co-owner have survivors' rights* _____

Money owed (amount, to whom, payment terms) _____

Repair person _____ Phone _____

LOCATION Location of ownership documents   _____
(pink slips/warranties/repair records/extra keys) _____

Additional information _____

_____⊗_____

Make, model, serial # _____

Purchase price _____ Date purchased _____

Purchased from _____

License # and state _____

Co-owner _____

Does co-owner have survivors' rights _____

Money owed (amount, to whom, payment terms) _____

Repair person _____ Phone _____

LOCATION Location of ownership documents   _____
(pink slips/warranties/repair records/extra keys) _____

Additional information _____

*Depending on the type of vehicle, how you hold this title and the rules of the state in which the vehicle is registered a co-owner may be a "joint tenant" or "tenant in common" in the vehicle. Co-ownership is discussed further in Part III, Step 9. Check your title slip and the rules of your state if you are a co-owner.

34

Make, model, serial # _____

Purchase price _____ Date purchased _____

Purchased from _____

License # and state _____

Co-owner _____

Does co-owner have survivors' rights _____

Money owed (amount, to whom, payment terms) _____

Repair person _____ Phone _____

Location of ownership documents
(pink slips/warranties/repair records/extra keys) _____

Additional information _____ _____

Net value of vehicles $_____ as of _____

G. Things of Value

This is where you list your tangible assets. These include everything from computers, jewelry, paintings and rare books to guns, coins, stamps, collectibles, antiques,
heirlooms and anything else of value. This is also where you list more ordinary
property, such as clothes and household furnishings. List valuable items separately.
Miscellaneous household goods and other property of minor cash value can simply be
listed by their total net worth. Things which have sentimental value but small mone-
tary worth should also be included.

We recommend that you take pictures of all valuable items. You may need them for
insurance purposes. And, at your death, they can be a big help identifying particular
items. If you do take photos, store them in a safe place and list that place below.

REMINDER: If you wish to keep the location of some items secure and secret, tear-
out the pages used to record these locations. Obviously, you should provide some
method to allow those who will handle your affairs to find these papers. You could, for
example, give the name and address of a person with whom copies of these pages have
been left, or put them in your safe deposit box. At any rate, in Section U be sure you
record where you put any pages you may remove.

HARE LOOMS

Valuable item/description _____

Purchase price _____ Date _____ Current net value _____

Additional information _____

Location of item itself _____

Location of important papers, receipts, photos, appraisals _____

_____

_____

Valuable item/description _____

Purchase price _____ Date _____ Current net value _____

Additional information _____

Location of item itself _____

Location of important papers, receipts, photos, appraisals _____

_____

_____

Valuable item/description _____

Purchase price _____ Date _____ Current net value _____

Additional information _____

Location of item itself _____

Location of in portant papers, receipts, photos, appraisals _____

_____

_____

Valuable item/description _____

Purchase price _____ Date _____ Current net value _____

Additional information _____

Location of item itself _____

Location of important papers, receipts, photos, appraisals _____

_____

_____

Valuable item/description _____

Purchase price _____ Date _____ Current net value _____

Additional information _____

Location of item itself _____

Location of important papers, receipts, photos, appraisals _____

_____

_____

Valuable item/description _____

Purchase price _____ Date _____ Current net value _____

Additional information _____

Location of item itself _____

LOCATION

Location of important papers, receipts, photos, appraisals _____

_____

_____

Valuable item/description _____

Purchase price _____ Date _____ Current net value _____

Additional information _____

Location of item itself _____

LOCATION

Location of important papers, receipts, photos, appraisals _____

_____

_____

Valuable item/description _____

Purchase price _____ Date _____ Current net value _____

Additional information _____

Location of item itself _____

LOCATION

Location of important papers, receipts, photos, appraisals _____

_____

_____

Valuable item/description _____

Purchase price _____ Date _____ Current net value _____

Additional information _____

Location of item itself _____

Location of important papers, receipts, photos, appraisals _____

_____

_____

Valuable item/description _____

Purchase price _____ Date _____ Current net value _____

Additional information _____

Location of item itself _____

Location of important papers, receipts, photos, appraisals _____

_____

_____

Miscellaneous items at home _____

_____

_____

_____

Miscellaneous items not at home _____

_____

_____

_____

*I instinctively like to acquire and store up what
promises to outlast me.*

— Colette

Additional information _____

_____

_____

_____

Estimated net value of items specifically listed above _____ as of _____

Estimated net value of miscellaneous items (clothes, furnishings, etc.) _____ as of _____

Ah, take the cash, and let the credit go.
— Edward Fitzgerald

H. Money Owed You

In this space list money owed you in the form of personal debts. If you own a small business, money owed your business will be identified in your business records (Section E).

Debts which can't be established by a written document are often hard to prove and still harder to collect, particularly if the person who made the loan is deceased. If you have made oral loan agreements, it's prudent to get them reduced to written documents and stored safely.

NOTE: It's not uncommon for one family member to advance money to another in a transaction which is not meant to be a legal loan, but where some repayment responsibility is assumed. Perhaps the person receiving the money accepts an obligation to repay if that becomes financially feasible, or understands that the amount of money owed will be deducted from his or her interest in the advancer's estate. Although such transactions do not create legal debts, you may want to note them here for future family clarity.

Name of person who owes you money _____

Address _____

_____

Amount of debt _____ as of _____

Terms of the loan _____

Co-signor/Guarantor (if any)* _____

Security agreement** _____

Location of loan document, security agreement, record of payment _____

LOCATION

Additional information _____

_____

Total amount owed you _____ as of _____

⊗

Name of person who owes you money _____

Address _____

_____

Amount of debt _____ as of _____

Terms of the loan _____

Co-signor/Guarantor (if any) _____

Security agreement _____

Location of loan document, security agreement, record of payment _____

LOCATION

Additional information _____

_____

⊗

*A co-signor or guarantor is a person who has agreed to be responsible for repaying the loan if the principal borrower defaults.
**"Security" here means any property which the lender can seize or foreclose against if the borrower defaults. This would include a second mortgage, for example. Any security agreement must be acknowledged and identified in the loan agreement. If it affects real property it should be recorded.

41

Name of person who owes you money_____

Address _____

_____

Amount of debt_____ as of_____

Terms of the loan_____

Co-signor/Guarantor (if any) _____

Security agreement _____

LOCATION Location of loan document, security agreement, record of payment_____

_____

Additional information_____ _____

_____

Name of person who owes you money_____

Address _____

_____

Amount of debt_____ as of_____

Terms of the loan_____

Co-signor/Guarantor (if any) _____

Security agreement _____

LOCATION Location of loan document, security agreement, record of payment_____

_____

Additional information_____

_____

Name of person who owes you money_____

Address _____

_____

Amount of debt_____ as of_____

Terms of the loan_____

Co-signor/Guarantor (if any) _____

Security agreement _____

 Location of loan document, security agreement, record of payment_____

_____

Additional information_____

_____

Debt: an ingenious substitute for the chain and whip of the slave-driver.

— Ambrose Bierce

I. Money You Owe

All of your debts must be paid following death, often before your property can legally be distributed to inheritors. Since the amount of most of your day-to-day obligations such as the phone bill or your Sears account change quickly, there is little sense in listing this information. What should be listed are your regular accounts and other obligations. All charge accounts, for example, should be listed by name, account number and others allowed to charge. If you have other obligations (aside from home, real property or vehicle loans covered in Sections C and F), such as promissory note to a relative or bank, you should supply more detailed information, including the name of the creditor, address, telephone number, person to talk to, co-signer(s), location of loan documents and proof of past payments.

a. Credit Cards and Charge Accounts

Account Name	Account Number	Others Who Can Use	Phone Number to Cancel	Location of Records

b. Major Obligations

Type of obligation (personal loan, promissory _____
note, lawsuit settlement)
_____

Account or identifying number _____

Owed to _____ Phone _____

Address _____

_____

Payment terms _____

Additional information _____

_____

Location of documents and proof of payments _____

———————————————⊗———————————————

Type of obligation (personal loan, promissory _____
note, lawsuit settlement)
_____

Account or identifying number _____

Owed to _____ Phone _____

Address _____

_____

Payment terms _____

Additional information _____

_____

Location of documents and proof of payments _____

Type of obligation (personal loan, promissory note, lawsuit settlement) _____

_____

Account or identifying number _____

Owed to _____ Phone _____

Address _____

_____

Payment terms _____

Additional information _____

_____

Location of documents and proof of payments _____

c. Routine Household Accounts

List bills which are due monthly or quarterly such as telephone service, electricity, garbage collection, water, newspapers, gardening, milk delivery, etc.

Name	Address	Service	Average amount

d. Other Regular Obligations

Here you can list any regular debts you want others to be aware of, from dues in golf courses or athletic clubs to an investment advisory service or medical or other bills you are paying over time. Also include any informal credit arrangements you may have with local merchants such as the butcher or mechanic.

Name _____ Phone _____

Address _____

_____

For _____

Payment terms _____

Additional information _____

Location of documents _____

Name _____ Phone _____

Address _____

_____

For _____

Payment terms _____

Additional information _____

Location of documents _____

Name _____ Phone _____

Address _____

_____

For _____

Payment terms _____

Additional information _____

LOCATION Location of documents _____

Name _____ Phone _____

Address _____

_____

For _____

Payment terms _____

Additional information _____

LOCATION Location of documents _____

Name _____ Phone _____

Address _____

_____

For _____

Payment terms _____

Additional information _____

LOCATION Location of documents _____

Name _____ Phone _____

Address _____

_____

For _____

Payment terms _____

Additional information _____

LOCATION Location of documents _____

48

Name _____ Phone _____

Address _____

_____

For _____

Payment terms _____

Additional information _____

Location of documents _____

Name _____ Phone _____

Address _____

_____

For _____

Payment terms _____

Additional information _____

Location of documents _____

e. Outstanding and Contingent Liabilities

List any lawsuit(s) you are involved in or claims made against you. Also, list any court orders/judgments you are responsible for, such as child support or alimony awards. Generally an estate is liable for minor children, while alimony (spousal support) obligations end at death. An estate is also liable for pending lawsuits as well as existing judgments. If you have any questions about this you should see a lawyer.

Lawsuit

Case name _____ Number _____

Court _____

Status _____

Lawyer's name _____ Phone _____

Address _____

_____

Additional information _____

Location of your lawsuit papers/documents _____

Court Orders/Judgments

Case name _____ Number _____

Court _____

Status _____

Name payable to _____

Address _____

_____

Terms _____

Lawyer's name _____ Phone _____

Address _____

_____

Additional information _____

Location of court papers, proof of   _____
payments, etc.   _____

f. Informal Debts

Perhaps you have borrowed money, furniture or something else substantial from a friend or a member of the family on an informal basis. If you want to acknowledge those obligations, note that information here.

Name of person from
whom you borrowed _____ Phone _____

Address _____

_____

Item _____

Amount or location _____

Terms or agreement _____

_____

As of _____

Name of person from
whom you borrowed _____ Phone _____

Address _____

_____

Item _____

Amount or location _____

Terms or agreement _____

_____

As of _____

Name of person from
whom you borrowed _____ Phone _____

Address _____

_____

Item _____

Amount or location _____

Terms or agreement _____

_____

As of _____

NOTE: We suggest in the estate planning material in Part III that you identify
particular assets that will be available to pay your debts. In addition, often it is wise to
specify a person who will be responsible for insuring that your debts will be paid as you

have directed. Otherwise, considerable confusion and delay, or even conflict between inheritors, can result. Inevitably, anticipating final debts involves uncertainties; you cannot be absolutely sure what the debts will be, or what your assets will be worth. Nevertheless, it is a sound idea to make your best estimate of those debts, and to set aside sufficient assets to pay them. One method can be to identify the order in which assets should be used to pay your debts. For example, "First, use my bank account at _____ bank; then, if necessary, sell my stock in _____ _____ company; then sell _____ real estate . . ." Make your final arrangements clear and binding by expressly including them in your estate plan (again, see Part III).

> *Life insurance — an ingenious modern game of chance in which the player is permitted the comfortable conviction he's beating the man who owns the table.*
>
> — Ambrose Bierce

J. Insurance

Gaining rapid access to insurance policies can be particularly important for those who will take care of your affairs. So, be sure to list all your homeowner, auto and medical insurance as well as life policies.

a. Life insurance

Policy # _____ Face value _____

Company _____ Phone _____

Address _____

_____

Broker (if any) _____ Phone _____

Address _____

_____

Type of policy (term, whole life,
double indemnity, etc.) _____ Expiration date _____

Beneficiary(ies) _____

Contingent beneficiary(ies) _____

Additional information _____

Location of policy _____

———————————— ⊗ ————————————

Policy # _____ Face value _____

Company _____ Phone _____

Address _____

_____

Broker (if any) _____ Phone _____

Address _____

_____

Type of policy (term, whole life,
double indemnity, etc.) _____ Expiration date _____

Beneficiary(ies) _____

Contingent beneficiary(ies) _____

Additional information _____

Location of policy _____

———————————— ⊗ ————————————

Policy # _____ Face value _____

Company _____ Phone _____

Address _____

_____

Broker (if any) _____ Phone _____

Address _____

_____

Type of policy (term, whole life,
double indemnity, etc.) _____ Expiration date _____

Beneficiary(ies) _____

Contingent beneficiary(ies) _____

Additional information _____

Location of policy _____

NOTE: There are a number of automatic life and disability insurance policies which cover you if tickets for travel are charged to a particular credit card (Mastercard, for instance) and death or injury occurs while on that trip. A list of those accounts and their conditions should be noted here.

Account   Terms and Conditions

_____

_____

_____

NOTE: Collecting on a life insurance policy is normally very simple. All that is necessary is to submit the appropriate claim forms, the original insurance policy, and a *certified* copy of the death certificate to the insurance company. There is no federal income tax imposed on the receipt of insurance proceeds, although there can be state income or death taxes assessed.

b. Homeowner's or Renter's Insurance

Type/Coverage _____ Policy # _____

Company name _____ Phone _____

Address _____

_____

Agent/Broker (if any) _____

Phone_____ Address_____

_____

Property covered _____

Principal risks insured against _____

Special coverage (if any) _____

Other information _____

Location of policy, special _____
coverage, photos of property, etc. _____

Type/Coverage _____ Policy # _____

Company name _____ Phone _____

Address _____

_____

Agent/Broker (if any)_____

Phone_____ Address_____

_____

Property covered _____

Principal risks insured against _____

Special coverage (if any) _____

Other information _____

Location of policy, special _____
coverage, photos of property, etc. _____

c. Medical Insurance

Type/Coverage _____ Policy # _____

Company name _____ Phone _____

Address _____

_____

Agent/Broker (if any) _____

Phone _____ Address _____

_____

Special coverage (if any) _____

Other information _____

Location of policy, _____

Type/Coverage _____ Policy # _____

Company name _____ Phone _____

Address _____

_____

Agent/Broker (if any) _____

Phone _____ Address _____

_____

Special coverage (if any) _____

Other information _____

Location of policy, _____

d. Vehicle Insurance

Vehicle covered _____

Type/Coverage _____ Policy # _____

Company name _____ Phone _____

Address _____

_____

Agent/Broker (if any) _____

Phone _____ Address _____

_____

Special coverage (if any) _____

Other information _____

LOCATION   Location of policy, _____

Vehicle covered _____

Type/Coverage _____ Policy # _____

Company name _____ Phone _____

Address _____

_____

Agent/Broker (if any) _____

Phone _____ Address _____

_____

Special coverage (if any) _____

Other information _____

LOCATION   Location of policy, _____

e. Other Insurance

Item covered _____

Type/Coverage _____ Policy # _____

Company name _____ Phone _____

Address _____

_____

Agent/Broker (if any) _____

Phone _____ Address _____

_____

Special coverage (if any) _____

Other information _____

Location of policy, _____

K. Survivors' and Retirement Benefits and Pensions

Your survivors' and retirement benefits can include income from a number of different areas, such as social security, personal retirement plans such as KEOGHS, IRAS, and ESOPS, vested pension plans (veterans, employees, and union) as well as rights in profit sharing plans or stock options from your job, etc. Because so many different types of plans exist, it is impossible to create the perfect series of blanks to record every type of information. So please remember it's your data and not our form which is important and don't hesitate to make modifications to suit your needs.

a. Social Security

The laws regarding social security will undoubtedly change over the next several years, although we expect basic provisions to continue which provide for benefits to minor children and spouses (former spouses to whom you were married for ten years also qualify), who do not have their own coverage. We suggest you record your specific information here and then check with your local Social Security office for the current policy when you or your family needs additional information.*

Your Social Security number _____

Current or last employer's name _____

Address _____

_____

If currently receiving benefits, what   _____
type (disability, retirement, survivors')
                                                _____

If receiving benefits, amount and terms _____

Additional information _____

Location of documents pertaining to social security rights and benefits (documents required may include marriage certificate, social security card, birth certificate, income tax records, etc.)

_____

_____

_____

b. Veteran's Benefits

Many benefits are potentially available to a veteran and his or her family. These may include medical coverage, burial reimbursement, burial in a national cemetery, pensions, educational support and others. If you served in the Armed Forces, you should contact your Veteran's Administration office to see if you or your family are entitled to any benefits.

Address of V.A. office nearest you _____

_____

Person to contact _____ Phone _____

*If you have any questions about your social security coverage see "The Sourcebook for Older Americans: Income, Rights and Benefits", by Joseph Matthews, Nolo Press

Branch of the service _____

Date entered _____ Date discharged _____

Service # _____ Type of discharge _____

Your current benefits _____

Survivor benefits _____

Income _____ Terms _____

Additional information _____

Location of military/veterans documents (separation papers, commen-
dations, etc.) _____

c. Other Survivor or Retirement Benefits

This section should include public or private survivors' or retirement benefits and any corporate, federal city or municipal pension plans for which you are eligible. Don't forget ESOPs and any other income from previous employers, which will be available to your survivors.

Type of benefit _____

Person eligible to receive benefits _____

Income _____ Terms _____

Person or office to contact _____ Phone _____

Other information _____

Location of documents pertaining
to benefit (pension, policies,
employment records, etc.) _____

Type of benefit _____

Person eligible to receive benefits _____

Income _____ Terms _____

Person or office to contact _____ Phone _____

Other information _____

Location of documents pertaining   _____
to benefit (pension, policies,   _____
employment records, etc.)
    _____

d. Your Own Retirement Accounts

Here you list the accounts you have set up for your retirement. Including KEOGHs, IRAs, annuities and any other arrangements you may have made.

Type of benefit _____

Location of account _____

Income or account status _____

Payment terms or conditions _____

Person to contact _____ Phone _____

Other information _____

Location of documents pertaining   _____
to benefit
    _____

Type of benefit _____

Location of account _____

Income or account status _____

Payment terms or conditions _____

61

Person to contact _____ Phone _____

Other information _____

Location of documents pertaining _____
to benefit   _____

Type of benefit _____

       Location of account _____

Income or account status _____

Payment terms or conditions _____

Person to contact _____ Phone _____

Other information _____

Location of documents pertaining _____
to benefit   _____

L. Location of Personal Documents and Tax Records

For both sentimental and practical reasons, people will want and need to know where your important papers are located. Here you should give the locations of any documents not specifically mentioned in earlier sections.

A tax audit will normally cover 1-3 years before your last filing date and you are required to keep your records for these years. The IRS, however, recommends you keep your records for 4 years. This in case you have a reason to income average (which covers 5 years). Records which should be kept include all documents which support information you include in your tax forms for the period — cancelled checks, receipts, W-2 forms, etc.

Something called a "Ten Year Averaging Form" is used for lump sum distribution of funds such as IRAs or pensions. You do *not* need your IRS records for this type of averaging.

A few other points to remember: If you fail to file an income tax return at all or willfully attempt to evade taxes, the tax may be accessed or collected at any time. You could, therefore, need records long after the normal record keeping period.

In the area of personal real property transactions some records may have to be kept for long periods. The basis price of a house is used to determine potential capital gains. The price is the purchase price, plus any amount paid for capital improvements to the property and less any casualty losses (storm, earthquake or other damage) or changes in property (you sell a portion of the land). This means all supporting documents should be kept until you have determined if there are any capital gains to be paid. This could mean keeping records for 30 years if you own a house for that long or you buy a series of houses during that time.

If you face this situation it's certainly a wise idea to keep a file on improvements and other costs soon after they occur. It will be no fun if you or someone in your family has to attempt to straighten out your records or find receipts on a deck or room addition built 20 years ago. Mistakes can certainly result in cost increased tax liabilities, something we all want to avoid.

For additional information on record keeping for tax purposes get ahold of publications 17 and 523 from the IRS.

a. Legal Papers

This is where you enter the locations of such legal documents as birth and marriage certificates, name changes, divorce, naturalization and adoption papers, etc.

Description of legal document	Location	Other information

b. Tax Records

Record the location of your federal, state and city (if appropriate) tax returns for the last six years, as well as the location of supporting documents, including checks and receipts, if they are kept separately. If it is not obvious from examining these documents, this is a good place to list your tax preparer, accountant and any other person who might be helpful in the event of tax difficulties.

Type of document	Tax Preparer's name, address and phone	Location

Additional information _____

_____

c. Educational and Career Papers

You may also want to list important personal documents such as religious records, diplomas, school or career awards, and other prizes or honors.

Description of material	Location	Other information

d. Your Medical Records

Your medical records may prove significant to future generations and you may want to include important ones. If you move or change dentists or physicians it's a good idea to have any of your medical records forwarded to your new doctors. Don't forget hospital records. Having these may avoid unnecessary or duplicating x-rays and access to a thorough medical history can be crucial to diagnosis and treatment.

Description of record	Location	Other information

e. Your Personal Memorabilia

If personal memorabilia such as letters, photos, albums, old scrap books, postcards or books are stored in out-of-the-way places, a description of the items and locations will be useful.

Description of item	Location	Other information

f. Your Address Book

Finally, don't forget about your address book unless its location is well-known and obvious.

 Location _____

M. Safe Deposit Box

Safe deposit boxes are a traditional place to store important documents. Often it is wise to rent a box in joint tenancy with a person you trust (discussed in Part III, Step 9). This provides prompt access to your papers if you become ill or disabled. Also, a joint tenant of a safe deposit box normally has the legal right to gain access to the box if the other owner is deceased. This can prevent troublesome delays in obtaining the deceased person's vital papers.

Bank name _____ Box number _____

Address _____

_____

Official to contact _____ Phone _____

Joint tenant _____

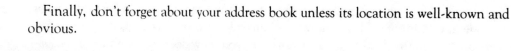 Location of key _____

Document location _____

List the contents or additional information _____

_____

_____

_____

_____

Bank name _____ Box number _____

Address _____

Official to contact _____ Phone _____

Joint tenant _____

Location of key_____

Document location _____

List the contents or additional information _____

_____

_____

_____

_____

N. Safe Places for Valuables

Here is where you put information about any storage places for documents or valuables not previously given. Presumably you have already listed your principal storage places, but there may be more. Don't forget unusual ones. For example, some people put silver, jewelry and other things in unpredictable places to gain some security. Record those places here so valuable items don't get lost or discovered by the wrong person.

Again, you might want to remove these pages. If you do, indicate where they may be found in Section U.

Item(s) stored _____

_____

Storage place/location _____

_____

_____

People to contact _____

_____

Additional information _____

Item(s) stored _____

_____

Storage place/location _____

_____

_____

People to contact _____

_____

Additional information _____

Item(s) stored _____

_____

Storage place/location _____

_____

_____

People to contact _____

_____

Additional information _____

O. Locks, Keys and Burglar Alarms

Here you should record information about your various locks, keys and other security systems. You don't want them to frustrate your own family and friends.

It is advisable to remove the following page and keep copies with someone in your family and a neighbor.

a. Keys

So many things in life use keys: lock-boxes, chests, cabinets, desks, houses, cars, boats, offices, storage sheds, freezers. Chances are you may have trouble recalling what some of your keys are for. If so, it's all the more reason to set up a system for those who will follow you. You may want to use a color code or number system, marking the key with tape and then recording which key goes to what.

Locked item	Locations (key & item)	Means of Identifying key	Other information

b. Combination Locks

Location of lock	Combination	Other information

c. Security Systems, Burglar Alarms

Where located _____

Operating instructions (tips, manual, code, etc.) _____

_____

Service agreement _____

Company to contact _____ Phone _____

Address _____

_____

Other information _____

Where located _____

Operating instructions (tips, manual, code, etc.) _____

_____

Service agreement _____

Company to contact _____ Phone _____

Address _____

_____

Other information _____

70

P. Property Maintenance

a. Property Maintenance Information

Much information about maintaining property can be lost if it is not recorded: up-keep methods for a cranky old summer home, the watering schedule for plants and gardens, or how to fix a perpetually balky machine. Likewise, the names and phone numbers of people who know how to repair your property, or who might know the real value of something you own, could prove very useful. This is your chance to pass on special information about your property. For example, if the boat won't start unless you kick it twice, and the boat repairman won't work unless you give him a six-pack on his birthday, write that down. If only one or two items of property need to be covered here, perhaps you can supply all the information required. Otherwise, you might note where more detailed information is located. The names of people who have repaired your property should be listed here. It also is a good idea to mark them in your address book.

Type of property _____

Location _____

Maintenance tips _____

Person to contact (name, address, phone,   _____
knowledge/purpose)
                                             _____

Additional information _____

Further information located _____

_____

⊗

Type of property _____

Location _____

Maintenance tips _____

Person to contact (name, address, phone,   _____
knowledge/purpose)
                                             _____

71

Additional information _____

Further information located _____

_____

_____ ⊗ _____

Type of property _____

Location _____

Maintenance tips _____

Person to contact (name, address, phone,
knowledge/purpose)

_____

_____

Additional information _____

Further information located _____

_____

Q. Location of Personal Property Loaned to Others

Personal property, from favorite books to lawn mowers, can get lost or forgotten if it has been loaned out, borrowed, or left in the custody of others. If any loaned property matters to you or might matter to your inheritors, listing its location will be a help.

Item of property _____

Location _____

Person to contact _____ Phone _____

Address _____

_____

Additional information _____

Item of property _____
Location _____
Person to contact _____ Phone _____
Address _____

_____

Additional information _____

Item of property _____
Location _____
Person to contact _____ Phone _____
Address _____

_____

Additional information _____

Item of property _____
Location _____
Person to contact _____ Phone _____
Address _____

_____

Additional information _____

R. Pets and Animal Care

During a lengthy hospital stay or following a death, the problem of who will care for any animals can be extremely worrisome. To avoid trauma both to animals you may have and to those who may not be properly prepared to care for them, we suggest you make careful arrangements in advance and record them here.

WAITING ROOM

Name of animal_____Species_____

Person to contact for animal care_____

Address_____

_____ Phone_____

Agreed upon arrangements_____

_____

Other information_____

Name of animal_____Species_____

Person to contact for animal care_____

Address_____

_____ Phone_____

Agreed upon arrangements_____

_____

Other information_____

Name of animal _____ Species _____

Person to contact for animal care _____

Address _____

_____ Phone _____

Agreed upon arrangements _____

_____

Other information _____

Veterinarian _____ Phone _____

Address _____

_____

Which animal(s) _____

Veterinarian _____ Phone _____

Address _____

_____

Which animal(s) _____

Veterinarian _____ Phone _____

Address _____

_____

Which animal(s) _____

S. People to Notify Immediately in an Emergency or at Death

The financial and practical information provided in the previous sections will be essential for anyone who must handle your affairs. It takes time, though, to resolve those matters. There is also a need to list, in one convenient place, all the people who should be notified immediately in the event of an emergency or your death.

a. Your Family, Friends and Neighbors

Name _____ Phone _____

Address _____

_____

Relationship _____

For what purpose or under what circumstances _____

_____

b. Your Family Doctor

Name _____ Phone _____

Address _____

_____

Your Specialist Doctor

Name _____ Phone _____

Address _____

_____

Specialty _____

c. Your Spiritual/Religious Counselor

Name _____ Phone _____

Address _____

_____

NOTE: Instructions about a memorial or funeral service are found later in this section.

d. Your Executor

Name _____ Phone _____

Address _____

_____

Your Contingent Executor

Name _____ Phone _____

Address _____

_____

e. People Who Will Care for Your Children*

Name _____ Phone _____

Address _____

_____

f. Your Employer

Name _____ Phone _____

Address _____

_____

---

*Appointing legal guardians for children's property and suggesting guardians for children in a will are discussed in Part III. Section C.

g. Your Business Associate(s)

Name _____ Phone _____

Address _____

_____

Name _____ Phone _____

Address _____

_____

Name _____ Phone _____

Address _____

_____

h. Your Attorney

Name _____ Phone _____

Address _____

_____

i. Other People (landlord, mortgage holder, banker, others)

Name _____ Phone _____

Address _____

_____

Purpose _____

Name _____ Phone _____

Address _____

_____

Purpose _____

T. Your Living Will or Power of Attorney

A living will is a statement which can be used if you would prefer not to have extended medical care if there is no hope of recovery. It does not have the force of the law in most states but it can be an important psychological factor in seeing that your intentions are carried out.

In some states there are legally binding documents you can prepare and sign which direct discontinuance of life support systems when you are terminally ill, and support equipment would only artificially prolong the moment of death. Under the Natural Death Act, you can sign a "Directive" which authorizes termination of life support equipment. Under an expanded form of the Natural Death Act or a "Durable Power of Attorney" you can give prior authorization to a friend or relative to authorize termination of life support equipment if you are so ill you are unable to act yourself.

If you plan to execute a living will, you might want to discuss the decision with your family. In most situations, if a family opposes a living will, their wishes will be respected. It is, therefore, important that your family and physician understand your feelings. If you decide on a living will you should have it witnessed by two people and copies should be kept with your family and doctor. It is also a good idea for you to review the contents regularly to be sure your thoughts have not changed. You can initial and date it after you have looked at it.

A copy of a widely used living will is included in Section III.

U. Things to Be Done at Your Death

Just as there are people who should be told promptly when you die, there are a number of things to be done. These include major tasks such as laying out your funeral plans and locating your will or other estate plans. They also involve some minor ones such as what to write on your headstone and what sort of obituary notice to send to the local paper.

a. Your Will

Do you have a will? _____

If yes, date executed _____

Location of will _____

Witness name _____ Phone _____

Address _____

_____

Relationship to you (employee, neighbor, other) _____

Witness name _____ Phone _____

Address _____

_____

Relationship to you (employee, neighbor, other) _____

Witness name _____ Phone _____

Address _____

_____

Relationship to you _____

Address _____

_____

b. Codicils

A codicil is a legal modification made subsequent to a will. If you have made any codicil(s), the specifics should be noted here.*

Do you have a codicil? _____

Since my will dated _____, I have executed _____ (a number) codicils.

---
*A new will might be preferable to a will with several codicils. If you have several modifications to an existing will you should review the matter with a lawyer.

The codicils were executed on the following dates _____

Location of codicils _____

c. Other Estate Transference Information

In Part III, Section C we discuss a number of types of trusts such as intervivos (living trusts), Totten, testamentary, revocable and others. If you establish any trusts you should complete the part below.

Have you established any trusts _____

If yes, date established _____

Type of trust _____

Name of trustee _____ Phone _____

Address _____

_____

Relationship of trustee (banker, financial advisor, other) _____

_____

Location of trust documents _____

Date established _____

Type of trust _____

Name of trustee _____ Phone _____

Address _____

_____

Relationship of trustee (banker, financial advisor, other) _____

_____

Location of trust documents _____

81

d. Body Disposition

There are a number of decisions which need to be made regarding the disposition of your body. In Part III, Section C we briefly discuss alternatives. And, it is probably easier for you to make them than members of your family.

Organ or Body Donation

Institution's name _____

Address _____

_____

Person to contact _____ Phone _____

Agreed upon arrangements _____

_____

_____

Location of documents (literature, instructions, other) _____

_____

━━━━━━━━━━━━━━━ ✖ ━━━━━━━━━━━━━━━

Institution's name _____

Address _____

_____

Person to contact _____ Phone _____

Agreed upon arrangements _____

_____

Location of documents (literature, instructions, other) _____

_____

Funeral Home, Burial Society, Funeral Society

Institution's name _____

Type of institution _____

Address _____

_____

Person to contact _____ Phone _____

Agreed upon arrangements _____

_____

_____

Institution's name _____

Type of institution _____

Address _____

_____

Person to contact _____ Phone _____

Agreed upon arrangements _____

_____

_____

Your Final Resting Place
   This should include whether you prefer, or have made arrangements, for burial,
mausoleum or cremation.

Lot, crypt, policy number _____

Location of documents (deed to burial _____
plot, perpetual care contract, prepaid
funeral plan, instructions to funeral _____
director)

_____

Funeral or Memorial Service
   Here you can specify if you would like a service, and, if so, where and what type.

Name of the place _____
(synagogue, church, funeral home, private home, other)

83

Person to contact _____ Phone _____

_____

Relationship (religious, friend, other) _____

Body present or not, open casket or not _____

Music, scriptures, poems desired _____

Pallbearers _____

Expense level preferred _____

Graveside service or ceremony with cremated ashes, other _____

_____

Headstone or other monument _____

Additional wishes or details _____

e. Obituary Notice

Why not try preparing your own? Create your own capsulized biography, perhaps including a favorite saying or philosophical view. You can also include a request that any donations be sent to a specific charity or institution. Newspaper obituaries normally go through undertakers, but it isn't mandatory. Alumni associations, clubs or professional journals could also be sent a copy.

Location of obituary, or include it here _____

_____

_____

_____

_____

Famous last words:

> *Now comes the mystery.*
> — Henry Ward Beecher

> *More light!*
> — Goethe

Into thy hands, O Lord, I commend my spirit.
— Columbus

Send to:

Name of publication or organization	Address	Attention	Additional information

f. Epitaph

This is a final opportunity for self-expression. If there is to be a headstone or plaque, why not create your own epitaph? For example, one of the authors has long since selected his epitaph, using the very words he used to respond to any parental order that he do some job; "RIGHT NOW?" Among our favorite epitaphs are:

Cast a cold eye, on life, on death. Horseman,
pass by!

— Yeats

and the classic:

On the whole, I'd rather be in Philadelphia.
— W. C. Fields

and the clever gravestone of J. Hallmark, London, England:

When you care enough to send the very best.

Your epitaph _____

_____

_____

J. Other Things to be Done

Here we reach the borderline between what really has to be done promptly and what can be left for a week or more. For those readers whose families will need to get the details of your affairs settled as promptly as possible we have a few more suggestions.

1. Cancel credit cards. All cards listed in Section I(a) should be cancelled. (Be sure a surviving spouse has a card in his or her own name.)

2. Terminate and get final accounting of information and credit arrangement with local merchants.

These should be listed in Section I(c). Provide any additional information here:

_____

_____

3. Other cancellations such as newspapers, periodicals, book/record clubs, other.

Name	Account number	Phone or Address

k. Promptly locate pages which have been removed from this book.

You may have removed information from this book because it was sensitive in a personal sense, or because you did not want the locations of your valuables lying around the house. Whatever the reason, you will want most of this information located promptly at your death. However, there may be certain people who you want to entrust this task to and others who you still would not want to have access. List any details here.

Page number	Location of original or copy	Person who may have access

Superfluous wealth can buy superfluities only. Money is not required to buy one necessary of the soul.

— Thoreau

Personal Memories
and Family History

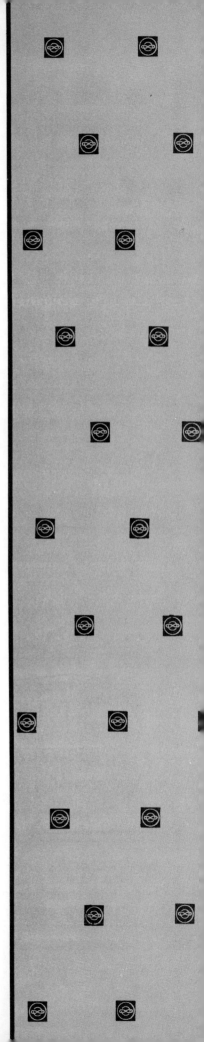

Introduction

Here in Part II we change pace. While your financial, business and household records set out in Part I are important, they are not the ties that hold a family together. For that you must look to basic things, such as where you and your family came from, who nurtured you as a child, who you laughed with, prayed to, learned from, loved and perhaps, even who you despised.

In other words, Part II offers you the opportunity to tell those who will come after you some of the events, relationships, joys and disappointments that defined you as a special person. Don't be afraid to tell the truth. All of us have a tendency to try and see the past in the best possible light. But this distortion of the facts is not what your family will want to know. Your great grandchildren, for example, will be as interested to hear just how scared you were on the Normandy Coast in 1944 as they will be to know you got the purple heart. And they may be more fascinated with the fact that you once ran away with an irresistable opera singer for a few weeks as they will be to learn that you later settled down and had four kids and a spotted dog named Harry.

We suggest that before you get out your pen, you glance through this entire section. For example, some of the subjects mentioned in Section A are covered again in Section D, Memories and Moments, where more room is allowed for comments.

A. Your Personal Data

Your Name

Your full name _____

Significance or derivation of your name _____

_____

Your Birth

Birthdate _____ Time _____

Weight _____ Place (city, county, etc.) _____

_____

Hospital name and location _____

_____

Details (hospital/home delivery, weather conditions, hours in labor, complications, drugs used, etc.) _____

_____

_____

Your Physical Characteristics

Natural hair color (age 20) _____ Eye color _____

Adult height _____ Adult weight (high/low) _____

Blood type _____ Shoe size _____ Ring size _____

> **A REMINDER:** There is more space provided in Section D, Memories and Moments, for additional information you may wish to provide for all of the items which follow in Section A.

Your Religious Beliefs

Religious affiliation _____

Your Ethnic Background

What countries did your various ancestors come from? _____

_____

A chart is a good way to see your roots. We have provided an example of one filled out and a blank for you to complete.

Stuart Toshiro McGrath			
⅜ English, ⅛ Norwegian, ¼ Irish			
1/8 Portuguese, 1/8 Japanese			

Maternal			Paternal
Mother	Parents		**Father**
1/2 English			1/2 Irish
1/4 Japanese			1/4 English
1/4 Norwegian			1/4 Portuguese

		Grandparents		
Mother	Father		Mother	Father
All English	1/2 Norwegian		1/2 English	All Irish
	1/2 Japanese		1/2 Portuguese	

		Great Grandparents		
Mother	Mother		Mother	Mother
English	Norwegian		Portuguese	Irish
Father	Father		Father	Father
English	Japanese		English	Irish

Maternal			Paternal
Mother	Parents		**Father**

		Grandparents		
Mother	**Father**		**Mother**	**Father**

		Great Grandparents		
Mother	**Mother**		**Mother**	**Mother**
Father	**Father**		**Father**	**Father**

Where You Have Lived

List places where you have lived, when you lived there and in a word or two what you were doing at the time.

Address   Dates   Reason

_____

_____

_____

_____

_____

_____

_____

_____

_____

Your Health

List major illnesses. It's possible that future research might establish presently unknown connections between heredity and certain diseases so be thorough.

_____

_____

_____

_____

_____

_____

_____

_____

Your Education

School names	Locations	Years	Degree/Grade completed

Your Occupations

List all your important jobs, but don't forget about some of the odd or special ones you may have had. If you picked fruit, ran a pasta machine or made two hundred pastrami sandwiches a day, put it down.

Company name	Job Title/Description	Years	Salary (high/low)

_____

_____

_____

_____

_____

Military Service

Although this is covered in veterans' benefits in Section I you might also want to list the information here.

Branch _____ Rank achieved _____

Dates of service _____

Places of service _____

Service number _____

Your Significant Relationships

Your marriage(s) (you can include live-in, common law, or other relationships)

Spouse/Other Name	Date married or together	Where married or together	Type of ceremony	Divorce/Death or separation date

B. Your Immediate Family

If you, or anyone in your family ever chooses to do genealogical research or develop a family tree, the kind of information contained in a chart like the one found here will be essential. And, even if it is never used for genealogical research, the records certainly will be of interest to others in your family. If you are like most of us, you will be amazed at how many people are related to you, if not by blood then by marriage.

To stir your memory, we have identified several generations of typical family members. The exact number in your family in most categories is, of course, impossible for us to predict. So, rather than allowing a set number of lines for you to fill in, we have left the selection of who and how many to include up to you.

NOTE: Relationships can get quite complicated these days with lots of families experiencing divorce, remarriage, adoption, half-siblings, etc. Make a note if someone is adopted, a step or half relationship, related to you by marriage or is on your maternal/paternal side of the family. Do the best you can to record as much as you can.

Family Members You May Wish to Include:

Great Grandparents
Grandparents
Parents
Brothers & Sisters
Spouse
Children
Grandchildren
Great Grandchildren

Aunts & Uncles — Maternal
Cousins — Maternal
Aunts & Uncles — Paternal
Cousins — Paternal
Nieces & Nephews

Other Significant Members of Your Family (include people who are not blood relations, but are an integral part of the family)

Relationship to you	Full Name (include maiden & married)	Birthdate	Date & Cause of Death

Relationship to you	Full Name (include maiden & married)	Birthdate	Date & Cause of Death

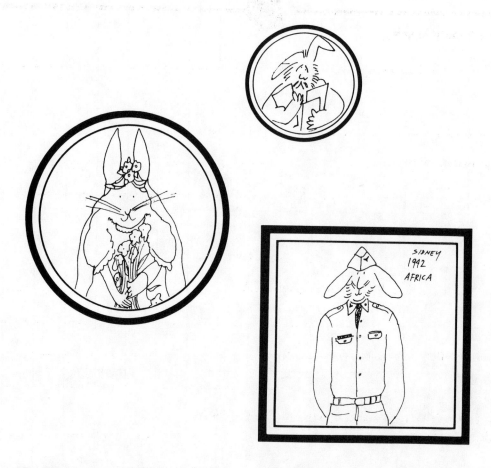

C. Personal Data — Your Immediate Family

There are so many things we don't know about the people who are part of our heritage and our blood. Black and white photographs may be the only image we have of people who died when we were young. Some of us have never even seen one or more of our close living relatives.

Think about your grandparents and great grandparents. Aren't there a surprising number of blank spaces you would like to fill in about their lives? Things ranging from height, shoe size, eye color and blood type to schools attended, jobs held, places lived and exciting tidbits about their lives.

While all sorts of interesting family history may be lost to you, you do have a chance to leave your descendants in a better position. Chances are you know much about a number of family members. As most of them probably won't make a record of their own history, you can do your existing and future family a great favor by functioning as the amateur family historian. This section is designed to that end. Think about those family members listed in Section B who you either know something about or who you can do some research about and record that information here.

Which people you choose to include is completely up to you.

Personal Data of a Family Member

Relationship to you _____

Name

Full name _____

Significance or derivation of name _____

_____

Birth

Birthdate _____ Time _____

Weight _____ Place (city, county, etc.) _____

_____

Hospital name and location _____

_____

Details (hospital/home delivery, weather conditions, hours in labor, complications, drugs used, etc.) _____

_____

_____

Physical Characteristics

Natural hair color (age 20) _____ Eye color _____

Adult height _____ Adult weight (high/low) _____

Blood type _____ Shoe size _____ Ring size _____

Religion

Religious affiliation _____

Places Lived

Where did the person live, when and why?

Address _____ Dates _____ Reason _____

_____

_____

Health

List major illnesses. It's possible that future research might establish presently unknown connections between heredity and certain diseases so be thorough.

Education

School names	Locations	Years	Degree/Grade completed

Occupations

Company name	Job Title/Description	Years	Salary (high/low)

_____

_____

_____

_____

_____

_____

Military Service

Branch _____ Rank achieved _____

Dates of service _____

Places of service _____

Service number _____

Significant Relationships

Marriage(s) (you can include live-in, common law, or other relationships)

Spouse/Other Name	Date married or together	Where married or together	Type of ceremony	Divorce/Death or separation date

Exciting Tidbits/Additional Information

_____

_____

_____

_____

Personal Data of a Family Member

Relationship to you _____

Name

Full name _____

Significance or derivation of name _____

_____

Birth

Birthdate _____ Time _____

Weight _____ Place (city, county, etc.) _____

_____

Hospital name and location _____

_____

Details (hospital/home delivery, weather conditions, hours in labor, complications, drugs used, etc.) _____

_____

_____

Physical Characteristics

Natural hair color (age 20) _____ Eye color _____

Adult height _____ Adult weight (high/low) _____

Blood type _____ Shoe size _____ Ring size _____

Religion

Religious affiliation _____

Places Lived

Where did the person live, when and why?

Address   Dates   Reason

_____

_____

_____

_____

_____

Health

List major illnesses. It's possible that future research might establish presently unknown connections between heredity and certain diseases so be thorough.

_____

_____

_____

_____

Education

School names	Locations	Years	Degree/Grade completed

Occupations

Company name	Job Title/Description	Years	Salary (high/low)

_____
_____
_____
_____
_____
_____
_____

Military Service

Branch _____ Rank achieved _____

Dates of service _____

Places of service _____

Service number _____

Significant Relationships

Marriage(s) (you can include live-in, common law, or other relationships)

Spouse/Other Name	Date married or together	Where married or together	Type of ceremony	Divorce/Death or separation date

Exciting Tidbits/Additional Information

_____
_____
_____
_____
_____

Personal Data of a Family Member

Relationship to you _____

Name

Full name _____

Significance or derivation of name _____

_____

Birth

Birthdate _____ Time _____

Weight _____ Place (city, county, etc.) _____

_____

Hospital name and location _____

_____

Details (hospital/home delivery, weather conditions, hours in labor, complications, drugs used, etc.) _____

_____

_____

Physical Characteristics

Natural hair color (age 20) _____ Eye color _____

Adult height _____ Adult weight (high/low) _____

Blood type _____ Shoe size _____ Ring size _____

Religion

Religious affiliation _____

Places Lived

Where did the person live, when and why?

Address   Dates   Reason

_____

_____

_____

_____

_____

Health

List major illnesses. It's possible that future research might establish presently unknown connections between heredity and certain diseases so be thorough.

_____

_____

_____

_____

Education

School names	Locations	Years	Degree/Grade completed

Occupations

Company name	Job Title/Description	Years	Salary (high/low)

_____
_____
_____
_____
_____
_____

Military Service

Branch _____ Rank achieved _____

Dates of service _____

Places of service _____

Service number _____

Significant Relationships

Marriage(s) (you can include live-in, common law, or other relationships)

Spouse/Other Name	Date married or together	Where married or together	Type of ceremony	Divorce/Death or separation date

Exciting Tidbits/Additional Information

_____
_____
_____
_____
_____

Personal Data of a Family Member

Relationship to you _____

Name

Full name _____

Significance or derivation of name _____

_____

Birth

Birthdate _____ Time _____

Weight _____ Place (city, county, etc.) _____

_____

Hospital name and location _____

_____

Details (hospital/home delivery, weather conditions, hours in labor,
complications, drugs used, etc.) _____

_____

_____

Physical Characteristics

Natural hair color (age 20) _____ Eye color _____

Adult height _____ Adult weight (high/low) _____

Blood type _____ Shoe size _____ Ring size _____

Religion

Religious affiliation _____

Places Lived

Where did the person live, when and why?

Address   Dates   Reason

_____

_____

_____

_____

_____

Health

List major illnesses. It's possible that future research might establish presently unknown connections between heredity and certain diseases so be thorough.

_____

_____

_____

_____

_____

Education

School names	Locations	Years	Degree/Grade completed

Occupations

Company name	Job Title/Description	Years	Salary (high/low)

_____

_____

_____

_____

_____

_____

_____

Military Service

Branch _____ Rank achieved _____

Dates of service _____

Places of service _____

Service number _____

Significant Relationships

Marriage(s) (you can include live-in, common law, or other relationships)

Spouse/Other Name	Date married or together	Where married or together	Type of ceremony	Divorce/Death or separation date

Exciting Tidbits/Additional Information

_____

_____

_____

_____

_____

Personal Data of a Family Member

Relationship to you _____

Name

Full name _____

Significance or derivation of name _____

_____

Birth

Birthdate _____ Time _____

Weight _____ Place (city, county, etc.) _____

_____

Hospital name and location _____

_____

Details (hospital/home delivery, weather conditions, hours in labor,
complications, drugs used, etc.) _____

_____

_____

Physical Characteristics

Natural hair color (age 20) _____ Eye color _____

Adult height _____ Adult weight (high/low) _____

Blood type _____ Shoe size _____ Ring size _____

Religion

Religious affiliation _____

Places Lived

Where did the person live, when and why?

Address   Dates   Reason

_____

_____

_____

_____

_____

_____

Health

List major illnesses. It's possible that future research might establish presently unknown connections between heredity and certain diseases so be thorough.

_____

_____

_____

_____

_____

Education

School names	Locations	Years	Degree/Grade completed

Occupations

Company name	Job Title/Description	Years	Salary (high/low)

_____

_____

_____

_____

_____

_____

Military Service

Branch _____ Rank achieved _____

Dates of service _____

Places of service _____

Service number _____

Significant Relationships

Marriage(s) (you can include live-in, common law, or other relationships)

Spouse/Other Name	Date married or together	Where married or together	Type of ceremony	Divorce/Death or separation date

Exciting Tidbits/Additional Information

_____

_____

_____

_____

_____

Personal Data of a Family Member

Relationship to you _____

Name

Full name _____

Significance or derivation of name _____

_____

Birth

Birthdate _____ Time _____

Weight _____ Place (city, county, etc.) _____

_____

Hospital name and location _____

_____

Details (hospital/home delivery, weather conditions, hours in labor,
complications, drugs used, etc.) _____

_____

_____

Physical Characteristics

Natural hair color (age 20) _____ Eye color _____

Adult height _____ Adult weight (high/low) _____

Blood type _____ Shoe size _____ Ring size _____

Religion

Religious affiliation _____

Places Lived

Where did the person live, when and why?

Address	Dates	Reason

_____

_____

_____

_____

Health

List major illnesses. It's possible that future research might establish presently unknown connections between heredity and certain diseases so be thorough.

_____

_____

_____

_____

_____

Education

School names	Locations	Years	Degree/Grade completed

Occupations

Company name	Job Title/Description	Years	Salary (high/low)

_____

_____

_____

_____

_____

_____

Military Service

Branch _____ Rank achieved _____

Dates of service _____

Places of service _____

Service number _____

Significant Relationships

Marriage(s) (you can include live-in, common law, or other relationships)

Spouse/Other Name	Date married or together	Where married or together	Type of ceremony	Divorce/Death or separation date

Exciting Tidbits/Additional Information

_____

_____

_____

_____

_____

118

Personal Data of a Family Member

Relationship to you _____

Name

Full name _____

Significance or derivation of name _____

_____

Birth

Birthdate _____ Time _____

Weight _____ Place (city, county, etc.) _____

_____

Hospital name and location _____

_____

Details (hospital/home delivery, weather conditions, hours in labor,
complications, drugs used, etc.) _____

_____

_____

Physical Characteristics

Natural hair color (age 20) _____ Eye color _____

Adult height _____ Adult weight (high/low) _____

Blood type _____ Shoe size _____ Ring size _____

Religion

Religious affiliation _____

Places Lived

Where did the person live, when and why?

Address   Dates   Reason
_____

_____

_____

_____

_____

_____

Health

List major illnesses. It's possible that future research might establish presently unknown connections between heredity and certain diseases so be thorough.

_____

_____

_____

_____

_____

Education

School names	Locations	Years	Degree/Grade completed

Occupations

Company name	Job Title/Description	Years	Salary (high/low)

_____

_____

_____

_____

_____

_____

Military Service

Branch _____ Rank achieved _____

Dates of service _____

Places of service _____

Service number _____

Significant Relationships

Marriage(s) (you can include live-in, common law, or other relationships)

Spouse/Other Name	Date married or together	Where married or together	Type of ceremony	Divorce/Death or separation date

Exciting Tidbits/Additional Information

_____

_____

_____

_____

_____

Personal Data of a Family Member

Relationship to you _____

Name

Full name _____

Significance or derivation of name _____

_____

Birth

Birthdate _____ Time _____

Weight _____ Place (city, county, etc.) _____

_____

Hospital name and location _____

_____

Details (hospital/home delivery, weather conditions, hours in labor,
complications, drugs used, etc.) _____

_____

_____

Physical Characteristics

Natural hair color (age 20) _____ Eye color _____

Adult height _____ Adult weight (high/low) _____

Blood type _____ Shoe size _____ Ring size _____

Religion

Religious affiliation _____

Places Lived

Where did the person live, when and why?

Address   Dates   Reason

_____

_____

_____

_____

_____

Health

List major illnesses. It's possible that future research might establish presently unknown connections between heredity and certain diseases so be thorough.

_____

_____

_____

_____

_____

Education

School names	Locations	Years	Degree/Grade completed

Occupations

Company name	Job Title/Description	Years	Salary (high/low)

_____

_____

_____

_____

_____

_____

Military Service

Branch _____ Rank achieved _____

Dates of service _____

Places of service _____

Service number _____

Significant Relationships

Marriage(s) (you can include live-in, common law, or other relationships)

Spouse/Other Name	Date married or together	Where married or together	Type of ceremony	Divorce/Death or separation date

Exciting Tidbits/Additional Information

_____

_____

_____

_____

_____

Personal Data of a Family Member

Relationship to you _____

Name

Full name _____

Significance or derivation of name _____

_____

Birth

Birthdate _____ Time _____

Weight _____ Place (city, county, etc.) _____

_____

Hospital name and location _____

_____

Details (hospital/home delivery, weather conditions, hours in labor,
complications, drugs used, etc.) _____

_____

_____

Physical Characteristics

Natural hair color (age 20) _____ Eye color _____

Adult height _____ Adult weight (high/low) _____

Blood type _____ Shoe size _____ Ring size _____

Religion

Religious affiliation _____

Places Lived

Where did the person live, when and why?

Address   Dates   Reason

_____

_____

_____

_____

_____

Health

List major illnesses. It's possible that future research might establish presently unknown connections between heredity and certain diseases so be thorough.

_____

_____

_____

_____

_____

Education

School names	Locations	Years	Degree/Grade completed

Occupations

Company name	Job Title/Description	Years	Salary (high/low)

_____

_____

_____

_____

_____

_____

Military Service

Branch _____ Rank achieved _____

Dates of service _____

Places of service _____

Service number _____

Significant Relationships

Marriage(s) (you can include live-in, common law, or other relationships)

Spouse/Other Name	Date married or together	Where married or together	Type of ceremony	Divorce/Death or separation date

Exciting Tidbits/Additional Information

_____

_____

_____

_____

Personal Data of a Family Member

Relationship to you _____

Name

Full name _____

Significance or derivation of name _____

_____

Birth

Birthdate _____ Time _____

Weight _____ Place (city, county, etc.) _____

_____

Hospital name and location _____

_____

Details (hospital/home delivery, weather conditions, hours in labor, complications, drugs used, etc.) _____

_____

_____

Physical Characteristics

Natural hair color (age 20) _____ Eye color _____

Adult height _____ Adult weight (high/low) _____

Blood type _____ Shoe size _____ Ring size ____

Religion

Religious affiliation _____

Places Lived

Where did the person live, when and why?

Address   Dates   Reason

_____

_____

_____

_____

_____

List major illnesses. It's possible that future research might establish presently unknown connections between heredity and certain diseases so be thorough.

_____

_____

_____

_____

_____

_____

School names	Locations	Years	Degree/Grade completed

Occupations

Company name	Job Title/Description	Years	Salary (high/low)

_____

_____

_____

_____

_____

_____

Military Service

Branch _____ Rank achieved _____

Dates of service _____

Places of service _____

Service number _____

Significant Relationships

Marriage(s) (you can include live-in, common law, or other relationships)

Spouse/Other Name	Date married or together	Where married or together	Type of ceremony	Divorce/Death or separation date

Exciting Tidbits/Additional Information

_____

_____

_____

_____

_____

Personal Data of a Family Member

Relationship to you _____

Name

Full name _____

Significance or derivation of name _____

_____

Birth

Birthdate _____ Time _____

Weight _____ Place (city, county, etc.) _____

_____

Hospital name and location _____

_____

Details (hospital/home delivery, weather conditions, hours in labor, complications, drugs used, etc.) _____

_____

_____

Physical Characteristics

Natural hair color (age 20) _____ Eye color _____

Adult height _____ Adult weight (high/low) _____

Blood type _____ Shoe size _____ Ring size _____

Religion

Religious affiliation _____

Places Lived

Where did the person live, when and why?

Address   Dates   Reason

_____

_____

_____

_____

_____

_____

List major illnesses. It's possible that future research might establish presently unknown connections between heredity and certain diseases so be thorough.

_____

_____

_____

_____

_____

School names	Locations	Years	Degree/Grade completed

Occupations

Company name	Job Title/Description	Years	Salary (high/low)

_____

_____

_____

_____

_____

_____

Military Service

Branch _____ Rank achieved _____

Dates of service _____

Places of service _____

Service number _____

Significant Relationships

Marriage(s) (you can include live-in, common law, or other relationships)

Spouse/Other Name	Date married or together	Where married or together	Type of ceremony	Divorce/Death or separation date

Exciting Tidbits/Additional Information

_____

_____

_____

_____

_____

Personal Data of a Family Member

Relationship to you _____

Name

Full name _____

Significance or derivation of name _____

_____

Birth

Birthdate _____ Time _____

Weight _____ Place (city, county, etc.) _____

_____

Hospital name and location _____

_____

Details (hospital/home delivery, weather conditions, hours in labor, complications, drugs used, etc.) _____

_____

_____

Physical Characteristics

Natural hair color (age 20) _____ Eye color _____

Adult height _____ Adult weight (high/low) _____

Blood type _____ Shoe size _____ Ring size _____

Religion

Religious affiliation _____

Places Lived

Where did the person live, when and why?

Address   Dates   Reason

_____

_____

_____

_____

_____

Health

List major illnesses. It's possible that future research might establish presently unknown connections between heredity and certain diseases so be thorough.

_____

_____

_____

_____

_____

Education

School names	Locations	Years	Degree/Grade completed

Occupations

Company name	Job Title/Description	Years	Salary (high/low)

_____

_____

_____

_____

_____

_____

Military Service

Branch _____ Rank achieved _____

Dates of service _____

Places of service _____

Service number _____

Significant Relationships

Marriage(s) (you can include live-in, common law, or other relationships)

Spouse/Other Name	Date married or together	Where married or together	Type of ceremony	Divorce/Death or separation date

Exciting Tidbits/Additional Information

_____

_____

_____

_____

_____

Personal Data of a Family Member

Relationship to you _____

Name

Full name _____

Significance or derivation of name _____

_____

Birth

Birthdate _____ Time _____

Weight _____ Place (city, county, etc.) _____

_____

Hospital name and location _____

_____

Details (hospital/home delivery, weather conditions, hours in labor, complications, drugs used, etc.) _____

_____

_____

Physical Characteristics

Natural hair color (age 20) _____ Eye color _____

Adult height _____ Adult weight (high/low) _____

Blood type _____ Shoe size _____ Ring size _____

Religion

Religious affiliation _____

Places Lived

Where did the person live, when and why?

Address	Dates	Reason

_____
_____
_____

Health

List major illnesses. It's possible that future research might establish presently unknown connections between heredity and certain diseases so be thorough.

_____
_____
_____
_____
_____
_____

Education

School names	Locations	Years	Degree/Grade completed

Occupations

Company name	Job Title/Description	Years	Salary (high/low)

_____

_____

_____

_____

_____

_____

Military Service

Branch _____ Rank achieved _____

Dates of service _____

Places of service _____

Service number _____

Significant Relationships

Marriage(s) (you can include live-in, common law, or other relationships)

Spouse/Other Name	Date married or together	Where married or together	Type of ceremony	Divorce/Death or separation date

Exciting Tidbits/Additional Information

_____

_____

_____

_____

_____

FIRST RIDE ON THE MERRY GO ROUND

D. Memories and Moments

Each of our lives are defined by many events, people and experiences. What is crucial to one of us may be insignificant to another. Creative energies and friendships surrounding your work may be extremely important. You may have found your moments of joy, comradeship or excitement in the activities of your church, lodge or garden club or climbing high mountains, hitting a golf ball or making a quilt. Whatever moved you in this life, this is the space to record it. We hope you will be as personal as possible. So, if you love bird watching, flyfishing, playing piano or being in love in the sunshine, this is your chance to sing about it.

We have listed a number of activities and subject areas which you may want to write about. We do this not because we think you should cover them, but because we found them to be fascinating subject areas when talking to our own families. You will undoubtedly think of things that mattered to you which aren't on our list.

Here is a tip we found helpful when writing about our families. Prepare and edit drafts of your writings before entering them in the book. If your experience is at all like ours, it will take some effort to find just the right words. If you need more space, continue your remarks in the blank pages in Part IV at the back of the book. Again, be sure to list the page number where your continuation appears.

Childhood: Who were your favorite friends? What games and sports did you play? What about experiences at camp? Any nightmares, imaginary friends, pets, boogie men?

_____

_____

_____

_____

_____

_____

_____

_____

_____

_____

_____

_____

_____

_____

_____

AND THEIR NAMES WERE JAUNTIN' JASCERT AND RANNIE TUTU AND...

SECRET PLACES   SECRET FRIENDS

JIGSAW PUZZLING WITH YOUR BEST FRIEND

Hobbies & Collections: From baseball cards to antiques. How did you start, how extensively involved did you become?

_____

_____

_____

_____

_____

_____

_____

_____

_____

_____

_____

_____

_____

_____

_____

_____

School: How do you remember yourself? Any honors, awards, scholarships? Were there any especially unpleasant and pleasant experiences, particular likes and dislikes?

_____

_____

_____

_____

_____

_____

_____

_____

_____

_____

_____

_____

_____

_____

_____

Mentors, Family & Friends: Who influenced you? Who were your favorite teachers, coaches, relatives? Were there people you admired or despised, who changed your life in some way?

_____

_____

_____

_____

_____

_____

_____

_____

_____

_____

_____

_____

_____

_____

_____

Family: Describe holidays, vacations, tragedies, the best and worst times, favorite gifts, childhood secrets.

_____

_____

_____

_____

_____

_____

_____

_____

_____

_____

_____

THE DAY YOU RECEIVED THE PURPLE TAIL FOR VALOR

Military: What were your friendships, fears, experiences? What activities do you associate with war or the military, whether you were in service or not?

Political: Think about the activities, beliefs and public figures who have affected your life. Any details about working in a political campaign or in a political movement?

_____

_____

_____

_____

_____

_____

_____

_____

_____

_____

_____

_____

Births: Give details about your children or things you may remember about your brothers/sisters being born. How about anecdotes or experiences during pregnancy, with miscarriages, infertility, special medication or medical treatments?

_____

_____

_____

_____

_____

_____

_____

_____

_____

_____

_____

_____

Sisters & Brothers: Any of those very special secrets? Games only you played? How about sibling rivalry or the closest you ever felt?

_____

_____

_____

_____

_____

_____

_____

_____

_____

_____

_____

_____

_____

Special Friends & Loves: Although we agree with the general rule that it is unfair to kiss and tell, historians are allowed a little license in this area. When did you first meet these special people in your life? What attracted you to them? Where are they today?

_____

_____

_____

_____

_____

_____

_____

_____

_____

_____

_____

_____

_____

Physical Changes: Growing up and growing older. When did you first begin menses, get whiskers, start shaving, have braces, begin puberty? What about wearing eyeglasses, getting bifocals, noticing grey hair, starting to lose hair, beginning menopause, having someone offer you a seat on a bus? When did someone first call you ma'am or sir?

YOU'VE GOT MUMPS ON YOUR CHEST...

THE DAY THEY PUT YOUR
TEETH IN JAIL AND GAVE
YOU YOUR FIRST TRANSISTOR
RADIO

149

Physical Characteristics: Are you big, small, husky or slight? Do you have any of the genetically determined characteristics such as double jointedness, mid digital finger hair, the ability to curl your tongue (lengthwise), wiggle your ears, scoliosis, connected or detached earlobes?

_____

_____

_____

_____

_____

_____

_____

_____

_____

_____

_____

_____

_____

Adventures & Travels: Any spectacular places you visited, mountains you climbed, caves you explored? What about adventures backpacking or travelling overseas? Do you have any special travel tips?

_____

_____

_____

_____

_____

_____

_____

_____

_____

_____

_____

_____

_____

Thrills & Chills, Things Precious & Intense: What triggered high emotions, intense fears, ecstacy? Which experiences influenced you the most strongly? Things which made you very proud, angry, embarassed, blissful?

> _Every man's intimate history is a contribution to universal history._
>
> — Anaïs Nin

_____

_____

_____

_____

_____

Arts & Aesthetics: This also could be called inanimate mentors and friends. What poems, books, television shows or personalities, films, works of art, music made a difference in your life?

_____

_____

_____

_____

_____

_____

_____

_____

_____

_____

_____

YOUR FAVORITE BOOK

Things You Miss: When we think back on the old days, there are plenty of things we don't miss but lots of things we do. What about streetcars, bobby sox, the Beatles, pegged pants, convertibles, ducktails, bobs, Cole Porter? Do you miss elegant things like sterling silver silent butlers, beveled mirrors, rolled top desks? Can you remember cheap gas?

_____

_____

_____

_____

_____

_____

_____

_____

_____

_____

_____

_____

Work, Jobs & Careers: Tell about your highs and lows, career aspirations, dreams fulfilled and unfulfilled? What have been your greatest accomplishments?

_____

_____

_____

_____

_____

_____

_____

_____

_____

_____

_____

_____

_____

Geography & Places: What were your favorite spots? Were they places where you lived or went in the summer? Where is the worst place you were ever stuck? The most unusual place you have been?

_____

_____

_____

_____

_____

_____

_____

_____

_____

_____

_____

_____

Holidays & Vacations: What experiences did you have with your family or without? What were the most memorable times, the best and the worst holidays?

_____

_____

_____

_____

_____

_____

_____

_____

_____

_____

_____

_____

_____

_____

_____

_____

Growing Up & Being Grown Up: How did you find out about sex and babies? Any amusing or painful misconceptions you might have had? What about your honeymoon experiences? Where did you first make love and what was it like? Any serious, romantic or funny moments you want to share?

FIRST KISS

_____

_____

_____

_____

_____

_____

_____

_____

_____

_____

_____

_____

_____

Skeletons, Scoundrels & Suspicions: Most families have some dark secrets, things that everyone suddenly stops talking about when kids or strangers approach. Do you know or suspect any?

_____

_____

_____

_____

_____

_____

_____

_____

_____

_____

_____

_____

_____

_____

Jokes, Quotes, & Anecdotes: What are some of your favorite sayings or jokes? What stories about friends and family are told and retold? Are there some in things told in another language?

OUR SONG

_____

_____

_____

_____

_____

_____

_____

_____

_____

_____

_____

_____

Practical Tips: What rules of thumb or tips can you pass on? Do you know about canoe repair, getting bread to rise, removing stubborn stains, keeping silver polished?

_____

_____

_____

_____

_____

_____

_____

_____

_____

_____

_____

_____

Important Ceremonies: Recall those special services or ceremonies, including mitzvahs (bar/bas), weddings, christenings, confirmations, initiations, graduations, ordinations. Include the names of people involved whether it be Monseignor McGuire, Reverend Miller or Rabbi Shapiro. And don't forget bridal attendants, godparents and ring bearers.

_____

_____

_____

_____

_____

Private Messages: It is often easier for us to say things to people in writing than in person. You may want to write some of these messages here or, as an alternative, write private notes, listing here where they may be found.

_____

_____

_____

_____

_____

_____

_____

_____

_____

_____

_____

_____

_____

_____

_____

_____

_____

_____

_____

_____

_____

_____

_____

_____

E. Maintaining Your Family Ties

Each family is unique; no outsider can prescribe inflexible rules for maintaining or strengthening family ties. What makes great sense to a person with a Polish background might not even be understood by those of Scandinavian or African heritage. One of the most enjoyable things about putting this book together has been asking people what they do to keep their families close. Some of the answers were familiar, as our families have long done similar things. Others were new to us.

Here are some of the activities, tricks and traditions families use to alleviate the fragmentation so inherent in modern life.

• Take plant cuttings or transplant outdoor plants which belong to someone in your family. (One of the authors recently took cuttings from a Christmas Cactus at least 100 years old which had belonged to her great grandmother. Parent and child plant are doing fine.)

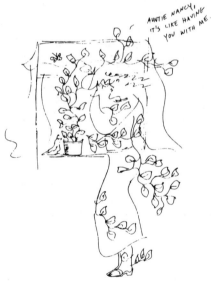

• Keep a record of the heights and weights of children. The birthday month is a good time to do this. One way is to write the figures in a permanent record book like this one but a more fun way is to draw the measurements on a wall or door. Of course moving can leave the evidence behind so you might want to plan in advance to someday trace the measurement lines and figures so you can take them with you.

• Make a keepsake/treasure chest. Like a time capsule, select items — photos, favorite toys or clothes, tapes, recorded messages on a day of celebration (wedding,

• Preserve old photographs. Mark as many as possible with the names and ages of the subjects as well as the year the photo was taken. Also, why not establish a pattern of taking family photos once a year at an occasion where many members of your family are normally present? Send copies to your entire family.

• As so many ads urge, use the telephone. If you cannot be face to face, voice to voice is the next best thing.

• You can't save a phone call, so don't neglect the art of letter writing. Consider organizing members of your family to write to you about their lives. Explain what you are doing and give people a reasonable time to respond. Collect all the responses and then, with everyone's permission, make copies and circulate them to interested family members. An even easier way to get this going may be to circulate a friendly series of questions to everyone. It is often easier to fill in blanks, even big ones, than to fill up blank pages. Another version of this approach is the round robin family letter. Instead of writing to all your family members individually, you write a letter about what has been going on with you, and send it to only one person in your family. That person adds their message, sends it to the next person and so on. When the letter comes back to you, you remove your original comments and substitute a new letter. Depending on the size of the family and the response time for each person, this can go on for weeks or even years.

• Maintain accurate addresses. Have someone take responsibility for maintaining current addresses for people and distributing them periodically. You never know when you might be traveling on business or vacation to a city which happens to be the new home of a favorite cousin you haven't seen in years.

• Collect recipes. Start to gather and exchange family favorites. Most people are flattered to know their potato salad, sushi or apple pie is something others think is special. There are blank cook books available for just this purpose.

GOOD FOR YOU BUNNIES...
PUTS PINK IN YOUR EARS...

GRANNY'S PRIZE WINNING CHUTNEY

birth, graduation) or that day's newspaper. Put these things away for a special occasion in the distant future to be given to one person or share the opening with the family.

• Pass on baby clothes and accessories among your own family. This might take some planning but there can be a wonderful connection when cousins, nephews and aunts share at least some of their clothes, toys or cribs.

• Try to keep furniture and other memory-laden items in the family. Unfortunately, items are often thrown away or given to strangers because no one seems to want them at the moment. When children first leave home parents commonly want, or need, to clean things out. This is often a time when children have neither the space nor desire for them. Later on a child may miss what now seems a treasure and be disappointed by its loss. The authors have both experienced this feeling. To combat this, try to notify people in your family well in advance if someone plans to "clean house." If an older person dies or suddenly moves from a longtime family home to a smaller space, consider chipping in to put their belongings in storage until there is time for others to pick out what they may regard as special.

• Frame trinkets and small treasures such as your grandfather's pocket watch, a baby dress, Uncle John's phi beta kappa key, Grandmother Amanda's gold-rim glasses, baby rings or shoes, young children's artwork or Aunt Clara's handmade doilies. These and lots of other things can serve as a decorative reminder of your past, instead of sitting in the bottom of a dresser drawer or cardboard box.

• Remember birthdays. Since most of us keep a calendar, it can be pretty simple to get a card in the mail or call once you have the dates recorded. It may make the person's day.

• Organize a family reunion. With determination and cooperation you can often get several people from around the country to the same spot at the same time. Perhaps a mix of holidays, business trips and short excursions in a car or van can get the family together. One of the authors comes from a family of seven children. Before our first reunion, Mom warned Dad, "seven adults, who used to be our children, are coming to stay with us."

• Record oral histories. The convenience of small tape recorders and cassettes makes it possible to preserve voices and stories. Don't just think of the older members of your family. The contributions and voices of children and even infants will also be a treasure. If you can't attend a family reunion send a tape. Be sure to label the tapes as to content and dates, and store them in in a secure place. Other members of the family should also know where they are kept.

• Keep a family album or scrapbook. In addition to a regular photo album, it can be fun to collect memorabilia such as favorite artwork by children, wedding or birth announcements, newspaper articles and photos or graduation programs.

• Recycle fabrics or entire pieces of clothing. For example, a silk shirt can be made into a man's tie or a scrap from a favorite piece of clothing can be made into a sachet. This takes planning and creativity, but the result can make a very special keepsake or gift. As for clothing, old styles periodically come back into fashion and your grandchildren may one day be delighted to wear your jewelry, vest or blouse.

• Put together a family tree (called a pedigree) and give copies to your family. There are many kinds of attractive preprinted forms for this purpose available at stationary stores or genealogical libraries.

Pedigree is from the Latin, *Pes* meaning "Foot" and *Grus* meaning "A Crane" because a pedigree chart resembles a crane's foot.

We invite you to send us any ideas you have to maintain family connections. We will make an effort to incorporate them into subsequent editions of *Your Family Records: How to Preserve Personal, Financial & Legal History.*

TRACING YOUR ANCESTORS

F. An Overview of Genealogical Research

We are the children of many sires, and every drop of
blood in us in its turn betrays its ancestor.
— R. W. Emerson

One increasingly popular family activity is genealogy, the recorded history of the descent of a person or family. Many find the process of genealogical discovery to be fascinating. Unfortunately, due to space limitations we can only present an overview of the field here. Should this perk your interest, however, we list a number of excellent works which will get you started on more serious genealogical research.

You may have the idea that thoroughly tracing your genealogy would be a time-consuming and complicated process. You're right, it can be. However, it's important to realize that the initial process of looking for your family's roots is not difficult. You probably know a great deal about your parents, grandparents and, perhaps, your great grandparents. Other family members may know more or different facts. Even recording this basic information will be valuable to those who come after you. Making a beginning doesn't mean you have to dedicate your life to the history of your family. You can choose to stop when you have either satisfied your curiosity, or become too frustrated. Maybe other family members will take over.

At this point we would like to pass on one important piece of advice from our parents, who have recently done genealogical investigations on our family backgrounds. "Start now!" Much can be lost by delay. In one of our families, an old trunk full of possibly vital papers was recently thrown out. In the other several relatives have died before the family memories they alone possessed could be recorded.

Start your research by locating a genealogical library. Chances are there will be one near you. A trip or phone call to your public library should give you the location. It may be at a university, church or public library; and there may well be more than one in your area. If so, each may have strengths in different areas (Jewish immigration to the U.S. before 1920, Native American Indians in the southwest during the 18th century, etc.) so your job will be to find out where to begin. Most genealogical libraries have extremely helpful and competent staff people, so don't hesitate to ask for help. Again let us remind you that we have included a list of good books on the subject at the end of this section.

Your initial reading should provide you an overview of the field, including the principal research methods and sources. As part of this you will be introduced to some specialized lingo. Fortunately, none of this is difficult. Indeed, many of the standard abbreviations, recording systems and forms can be mastered quickly. They work so well, there's little need for you to invent your own. From your initial reading, you will also learn how to handle common problems such as misspellings, name changes, conflicting information, re-marriages and step-children. If you don't already know what it means to be a first cousin two or three times removed, you will before you finish.

Another beginning step is to talk to the other members in your family, particularly older people. Collect whatever you can of oral memories, photo albums, letters, diaries, official records and newspaper clippings. Send letters requesting information. After a trip or two to the library you should have many specific questions to ask your family. Don't forget to share what you learn. You may inspire other family members to help. If others get involved in your search for your family's past, it may bring you closer together in the present.

Assuming you do get more deeply involved, you'll find there are many resources for further research. A number of organizations like The Church of Jesus Christ of the Latter Day Saints and other ethnic and religious genealogical societies have collected prodigious amounts of material. Most of this is available at little or no charge. Because genealogy is central in the Mormon religion, the Genealogical Society of Utah is one of the best. And, with 400 LDS branches throughout the world, you are probably within easy access to their printed records, microfilm library and educated staff. The Genealogical Society of Utah has already identified and processed close to seventy million names. This information is available to you whether or not you are a member of the Mormon church.

There are also a number of institutional and government records which probably will prove valuable in your research. For example, birth, marriage, military service, adoption, arrest, land purchase, probate, tax, immigration, naturalization and death records are all maintained by one or another public agency. Census records for the United States go back to 1790 and can be extremely helpful. Church, club, hospital bank and cemetery records are also commonly available.

Another avenue to consider if you exhaust your own energies or resources is hiring a professional genealogical researcher. You can often obtain significant results for as little as $50 to $250. Obviously you will get the most for your money if you supply good family background information and are specific about your requests. A librarian at a genealogical library can probably recommend a competent researcher. You may also choose a researcher from a list of registered genealogists. All states and most counties have a genealogical society and they would be able to provide you with the list. If you do hire a researcher, be sure to ask for references and then check them. Many genealogists specialize in a particular area, which can be geographical or by subject, such as naturalization records or a time in history. One word of warning here. Be wary of people who claim to do research and guarantee to provide you with your family crest. From our interviews, this seemed to be an area where many consumers are mistreated.

Genealogical research can lead to many pleasant surprises and wonderful connections as well as to an occasional family skeleton. One of the authors found out almost simultaneously she was related to Vidkum Quisling (a Nazi collaborator in Norway whose name has become synonomous with the word traitor) as well as to an early 17th century chaplain to the Norwegian royal court.

> *Examine well your blood.*
> — W. Shakespeare

> *What signified knowing the names, if you know not the nature of things.*
> — R. W. Emerson

In addition to the information in this book, I have the following genealogical records:

Items _____

Location _____

Items _____

Location _____

Items _____

Location _____

Suggestions for Reading About Genealogical Research

There are many wonderful books which will help you if you choose to do genealogical research. This is by no means a complete list. Some of the books here are small paperbacks and relatively inexpensive, while others are 1000 page hardcover books and quite costly. We hope, if you want to start any research, that these books will be of some help.

Preserving Your American Heritage, Norman E. Wright, Brigham Young University Press

The Handy Book for Genealogists, The Everton Publishers, Inc.

The Researcher's Guide to American Genealogy, Val D. Greenwood, Genealogical Publishing Co., Inc.

Genealogy as Pastime and Profession, Donald Lines Jacobus, Genealogical Publishing Co., Inc.

The Genesis of Your Genealogy, Elizabeth L. Nichols

How to Find Your Family Roots, T. F. Beard, McGraw-Hill Book Co.

Genealogical Source Handbook, George K. Schweitzer

Guide to Genealogical Research in the National Archives, National Archive Trust Fund Board

How to Trace Your Family Tree, American Genealogical Research Institute

Searching for Your Ancestors, Gilbert H. Doane, University of Minnesota Press

Genealogical Research—Methods and Sources, Milton Rubicam, Editor, American Society of Genealogists

Know Your Ancestors, Ethel Williams, Charles E. Tuttle Co.

The Genealogical Helper, Periodical, The Everton Publishers, Inc.

PART III

Transferring Your Property: Estate Planning, Including Wills, Probate Avoidance, and Taxes

A. Estate Planning for People Who Hate the Thought of Estate Planning

Estate planning means preparing for the practical consequences of a death, primarily transferring property to inheritors. In legalese, a person who has died is a "decedent"; a decedent's property, of whatever value, is his or her "estate." In the United States, there can be different tax, economic or other consequences, depending on which methods are used to transfer an estate. The main purpose of estate planning is to determine the most desirable transfer methods for your specific situation and needs.

Some people engage in estate planning in minute detail, while others ignore it altogether, an understandable attitude, but not a wise one. If you do no planning, your property will be distributed as state law dictates. This is unlikely to coincide precisely with your wishes. Still, we've found that many people simply can't bear to consider the rules concerning transfer of their property after their death. If you are in this category, we urge that, at a minimum, you prepare a will or alternate estate plan, or have a lawyer prepare one for you. Nolo Press provides resources which enable anyone to draft their own will, by using WillWriter, a computer program that runs on most small computers or, if you are not yet up and running through the computer age, *The Simple Will Book*. If you're unwilling to draft your own will or adopt one of the other estate planning devices discussed below, you'll need a lawyer. But even when prepared by a lawyer, preparing the paperwork necessary to transfer your property to your inheritors when you die doesn't have to be costly or time-consuming.

Where possible, we believe in a self-help approach to law. The balance of this chapter is devoted to an introduction to the basic concepts of estate planning. You can evaluate your own situation, and decide whether you want to try to do some of your own estate planning. But, if you find you simply can't stand the thought of planning your own estate, this approach is clearly not for you. And though we're normally reluctant to direct people to lawyers, at least not until they thoroughly understand their legal situation and the range of sensible legal choices, we want to say one thing loud and clear: better the cost of a lawyer-prepared will than no will at all.

CAUTION: A will is an efficient way to transfer property at death. However, property transferred by will normally goes through probate, a costly, time-consuming legal process which we describe further in Step 3. Probate can generally be avoided or minimized by proper estate planning. Depending on your situation and personality, it may make sense to consider doing this. In many situations, using both a simple will and one or more probate avoidance devices makes excellent sense.

B. Introduction to Estate Planning

Here we provide you with a step-by-step overview of estate planning so you can determine if you wish to go further in that direction. Unfortunately, we do not have space to present and discuss the laws of each state, nor the forms you need to prepare an actual estate plan. Still, this material should give you a good idea of what you want to achieve by your estate plan. We suggest you read all this material through once to get the whole picture before trying to make any decisions.

> *No lessons seems to be so deeply inculcated by the experience of life as that you should never trust experts.*
>
> — Lord Salisbury

Fortunately, estate planning for people with average or moderate-sized estates doesn't have to be forbidding or expensive. Many people can learn to do much, or occasionally all, of their own estate planning, thereby reducing costly attorneys' or other professionals' fees, or eliminating them altogether. Even those who will eventually turn the responsibility for their estate plan over to an attorney will benefit by a thorough understanding of what's involved. To get your money's worth from an attorney there is no substitute for being an informed consumer. We discuss the advisability of having your work checked by a lawyer in Step 15, below.

The Goals of Estate Planning

There are two basic goals of estate planning:

1. to gather factual information regarding one's assets, property and debts;
2. to decide on, and create, the most desirable legal method(s) to transfer that property to inheritors.

Gathering factual information is a practical matter. When a person dies, his or her property must be ascertained and collected, and any federal or state death taxes paid. All creditors must also be paid.

Assuming you have completed Part I of this book, you should have all the factual information normally needed to create a sound estate plan.

Deciding on and creating the most desirable methods for the transfer of your property requires that you understand the basic legal elements of estate planning, including death taxes, gift taxes, probate, probate avoidance methods, and wills. But simply knowing a little about each of these isn't enough. You need to understand how they fit together. For example, you may think that having a will is desirable. But before you trot down to your neighborhood lawyer to have one prepared, take stock of the information in this section about probate avoidance, and be sure that transferring all your property by a will truly fits your needs.

NOTE ON BOOKS AND SOFTWARE: Here at Nolo Press we have been writing and rewriting good self-help material (both books and software) concerning wills and estate planning for approaching two decades. We believe that the material we publish is the best available. In the next few pages, we will refer to it and recommend it several times. You may wish to assume that when it comes to our own material, we are self-interested, if not biased. This is a reasonable and healthy assumption, but we believe that if you are satisfied with this book, you will also be pleased with our other publications. If you are not, we will cheerfully refund your purchase price.

C. How to Create Your Estate Plan (An Overview)

Step 1: Determine what you have in your estate

You have already completed the first step of estate planning. This, of course, is figuring out what kinds of property you have and expect to own when you die. In Part I you listed items like pensions, insurance policies, stocks, personal effects, and bank accounts. All this taken together is your estate. For the rest of this chapter, you should have the results of your earlier labors in this book firmly in mind (and in sight as well), since the following discussion will ask you questions about your estate.

Step 2: Decide who you want to inherit your property and when

Focus on your actual desires without regard to whether they are wise from a tax planning or probate avoidance standpoint. Those matters will be addressed later. Who do you wish to inherit your property? Many people cannot answer this question in a single sentence. Often there is a great variety of property and many different inheritors. For instance, you may wish to leave the bulk of your jewelry to your daughter, but a specific bracelet to your grandson; your furniture to a son, except for a special rosewood table that will go to your niece Clarissa.

If you are seriously thinking about planning your estate, it is advisable to start sorting out questions now. To help you do this, we provide a worksheet where you can organize your thoughts by listing your property from Part I, and matching items with the name(s) of the person(s) you want to inherit it. Any person can inherit. So can corporations, which are considered by law (and in this book), as persons.

You can disinherit your children so long as you make it clear this is what you want to do. A number of states do not let you disinherit a spouse, however, unless you have adequately provided for him or her in other ways. The rules in this area are discussed in some detail in *The Simple Will Book* by Denis Clifford and the manual which accompanies the WillWriter computer program. In addition, people who wish to disinherit a spouse should generally have their estate plan checked by a lawyer.

Before you start on the worksheet, however, we want you to consider two additional questions:

1. Are you willing to transfer some of your property while you're alive?

2. Are you willing to partially commit some of your property to your eventual heirs while you're alive, even though you would maintain control and possession of the property?

These questions can be extremely important for estate planning purposes. As we see later on, there are often significant advantages to giving away your property while you're living, rather than having it show up in your estate and/or go through probate. Setting aside financial consequences for the moment, we simply ask you to consider whether you are willing to relinquish control of any of your property now, instead of later. The worksheet, therefore, has a space where you can put an "N" for now or an "L" for later.

173

WORKSHEET

Item of property	Inheritor	N/L	Net value

*There is no art which a government
sooner learns . . . than of draining money from
the pockets of the people*

— Samuel Smiles

Step 3: Learn the basics of tax planning and probate avoidance

1. Reduce Estate Taxes

Lengthy books have been written about estate taxes and tax planning. We can only present the basics here. Those readers with large estates will need the help of experts.

All property owned by you when you die, whether your share of ownership is 100% or less, is subject to federal estate tax. This property is conveniently termed your "taxable estate." Sometimes, as we shall see, you can avoid having a portion of your estate go to the federal government if you dispose of it while you are living. However, if you plan to do this, you will need to understand that there are also federal gift taxes and will want to understand how much you can give away each year and be exempt from these taxes (see Step 5, below).

Federal estate tax is based on the net value of your estate (market price less all amounts owed) as of the date of your death. You can readily determine the total present net value of your estate from the information listed in Part I.

The Estate Tax Credit

A rather large portion of your taxable estate is exempted from federal taxes by way of a "tax credit" which forgives estate taxes on amounts up to a certain set limit. This tax credit (usually called an "exemption") is $192,800. This means $600,000 can be transferred to your inheritors tax free.*

While this credit or exemption appears generous, there can be a catch. If your taxable estate is worth *more* than the federal estate tax exemption amount, the balance will be taxed at the rate applicable to the *total value of the entire estate.* Because the federal estate tax is graduated (i.e., the more money in the estate, the higher the tax rate), this rule means that your extra amount of property will be subject to a higher tax than if it represented your entire estate. We know this is hard to follow, but a concrete example should help.

EXAMPLE: Harry dies in 1988, with an estate worth $750,000. Because of the estate tax credit, $600,000 of the estate is exempt. Thus, $150,000 is subject to tax. The tax rate applied to the extra $150,000, however, is that for an estate of $750,000, and not for an estate of $150,000. The tax rate for $750,000 is 39%, whereas the rate for $150,000 if 32%.

---

*For more information about federal estate taxes, obtain a copy of "A Guide to Federal Estate and Gift Taxation," IRS Publication No. 488, available at most IRS offices.

The conclusion is obvious. If any part of an estate will be subject to federal tax, it is very desirable to find methods to reduce the estate to a point below the exemption amount, if possible.

The Marital Exemption

All money/property left to a surviving spouse is exempt from federal estate tax. This is called the "marital exemption."

EXAMPLE: Arlene Stein dies in 1988 with an estate of $1,300,000. She leaves $500,000 to her husband. There is no federal estate tax on this sum because of the marital exemption. She leaves the remaining $800,000 to her two children. Of this sum, $600,000 is exempt under the estate tax credit. So only $200,000 of the money transferred to the children is subject to federal estate tax.

Here too, however, the benefits are often not all that they might seem. Despite the fact that the marital exemption seems liberal, it can sometimes boomerang. If, for example, your surviving spouse is elderly, you may create future tax difficulties by leaving him or her a large amount of property.Why? Because his or her estate will then become subject to taxation on your combined property and the total tax will be larger than the sum of the taxes on your individual estates, due to the graduated nature of the tax.

EXAMPLE: Alfred and Loretta Gwynne each have assets of $425,000. Alfred dies in 1988. If he leaves his property to his children, there is no federal tax liability because of the estate tax credit ($600,000). Likewise, if he leaves his property to Loretta, there are no federal taxes owed, because of the marital exemption. But suppose he leaves his property to Loretta and she dies in 1989 with a total estate of $850,000, all of which is left to her children. Of her estate, $600,000 is exempt from federal tax because of the tax credit. Thus, $250,000 is subject to federal tax. Remember, there would have been no federal tax at all if Alfred had originally left his property to the children.

To avoid what estate planners call this "second tax" on larger estates, the first spouse to die can leave his or her property directly to children, grandchildren or whomever else will eventually wind up with it. Of course, if the surviving spouse needs the property, then some other plan will have to be adopted. One option is to create a trust (see Step 7), with the surviving spouse receiving the income of the trust for life and the property then going to the heirs who are ultimately to receive it. Under this approach, the money or property in the trust will not be included in the estate of the second spouse to die.

As we mentioned, one way to get your property down below the federally taxable amount is to transfer some of it while you're living. Of course depriving Uncle Sam of taxes is never simple. Here's the rub. If you give away property above a certain value, two things happen, both of which are closely related to the federal estate tax. First, you are taxed on the gift at the same rate as would apply if the property were in your estate upon your death. Second, you must use up the appropriate part of your estate tax credit on such a gift.

While we cover gifts in detail later on, we want to stress one point here: There may be better ways than gifts to reduce federal estate taxation. We discuss these methods later. Stay tuned.

State Death Taxes

The laws regarding death taxes vary widely from state to state. Even the names vary, with "inheritance tax" and "estate tax" being the most common. Some states, such as California or Nevada, have abolished death taxes altogether. Others exempt far less from taxation than does the federal government. However, all state tax rates (that is, the percentage rate applied to the total which is taxed) are much lower than federal rates.

Thorough estate planning includes learning about your state's death taxes. One reason for this is that property often cannot be transferred to inheritors until state death tax liens have been paid and released, a process that requires both paperwork and time.

2. Avoid Probate

Although all property owned by you when you die is included in your taxable estate (i.e., is potentially subject to federal estate tax), your property does not necessarily have to pass through probate. If some portion of it does, it is called your "probate estate." The higher the value of your probate estate, the bigger the bite taken by the lawyers will be. The fees charged by lawyers for handling probate are generally based on the gross value of the probate estate.* Thus, the smaller your probate estate, the lower the attorneys' fees and costs. So, in most cases, it is preferable to limit the amount of your property that passes through probate, or to avoid probate altogether.

The very word "probate" has acquired a notorious aura. While many people aren't sure what it is, except that lawyers and courts are involved, they certainly know they want to avoid it. That's a sound instinct. Probate is a costly, time-consuming business which can be greatly reduced, and sometimes even eliminated, through sensible estate planning.

What is probate? Probate is the word given to the legal process which includes filing the will of a decedent with the local probate court, locating and gathering the decedent's assets, and paying all legal debts, taxes, probate costs and legal fees. When all of that is done, the probate process is completed by distributing what's left as the will directs. If there is no will (and no probate-avoidance transfer method was used), the estate will undergo probate through similar legal proceedings called "intestacy" proceedings, and the property will be distributed as state law requires. Either way, probate commonly takes a year or more to complete.

NOTE: In some states, probate is not required (or there is a very simplified version of probate) for small estates or for money and property transferred from one spouse to another.

You may have noticed that most probate functions are essentially clerical. In the vast majority of probate cases, there is no conflict or litigation. Why then are courts and lawyers necessary? The reality is that as a result of several quirks of England's medieval history, English lawyers latched onto probate. American lawyers were quick to follow. Once lawyers get hold of any business, certainly one as lucrative as probate, it's very hard to pry it away from them. Over the years, American lawyers have invented various rationalizations to justify their continued control of probate. Most don't make sense.

---

* In California, Nolo Press publishes *How To Settle A Simple Estate* by Julia Nissley, a book which shows the layperson how to probate an estate, step-by-step and contains all the forms necessary to accomplish it.

In England, a greatly simplified, far less expensive, non-court probate system was adopted way back in 1926. We feel that the time for the United States to follow suit is long overdue. In the meantime, there is quite simply no good reason for you to subject your estate to the cost and delays of probate when it can be readily avoided. Transferring property outside of probate not only saves attorneys' fees, it also saves considerable time. Probate takes months, often years. By contrast, non-probate transfers can often be accomplished in a few days or weeks.

What specifically are these non-probate transfers? The main ones are owning property in "joint tenancy," use of a simple trust, called a "living" trust, and certain types of bank accounts. Later on, we explore each major type of non-probate transfer.

Step 4: Decide whether you are interested in pursuing estate planning further

Some of you have no doubt been pondering the question of whether or not to pursue estate planning further. Hopefully, most of you are still with us. Up to now, all we've explained is that there are advantages to planning for your property before you die, so that more of it will be left for your inheritors. However, you may not be ready to go deeper into estate planning, or you may want to leave this whole matter up to a lawyer without further concern on your part. If so, we suggest you turn to Step 12, which covers wills. If you want to gain a deeper understanding of estate planning, read on as we explore in more detail ways to reduce estate taxes or avoid probate.

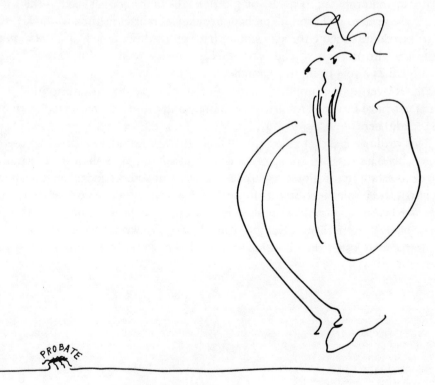

Step 5: Understand how gifts can be used to reduce taxes and avoid probate

Basically, a gift is any transfer of property that is not commercial in spirit. Property which has been legally given away cannot be part of the giver's taxable or probate estate. However, the giver of a gift is subject to federal, and often state, gift tax based on the market value of the gift. You may think only Scrooge would tax gifts, but there is sound reason for it. If there were no gift taxes, anyone (and everyone) could escape estate taxes entirely, simply by giving away their property before death.

To understand the ways gifts can be used in estate planning, you have to comprehend gift tax laws. Let's get down to some specifics.

First, gifts totalling $10,000 per year (or less) given to any one person or institution are exempt from federal gift tax. With a married couple, each spouse has a separate $10,000 exemption. This means the maximum a couple can give, tax free, to any other person is $20,000 per year. There is no limit on the number of persons or institutions which may be given tax free gifts per year. In other words, you could play Santa Claus and give many $10,000 gifts ($20,000 if you gave as a couple) to separate recipients each year without paying a penny of tax.

Second, all gifts from one spouse to another are exempt from gift taxes.

Third, the same tax credits, exemptions, and tax rates that apply to federal estate taxes also apply to gift taxes. The IRS takes the position that use of the tax credit is mandatory, not optional.

EXAMPLE 1: Pam gives her granddaughter $50,000. Of the gift, $10,000 is exempt from gift tax because of the annual exemption. The remaining $40,000 is subject to gift tax. The IRS requires that, rather than paying the amount of tax, which is $8,200, Pam must use up $8,200 of her estate/gift tax credit. Thus, when Pam dies, her estate will be able to transfer $40,000 less without paying estate tax that would have been possible if the gift had not been made.

EXAMPLE 2: Now let's assume Pam gives her granddaughter the same $50,000, but spreads it out over five years at $10,000 per year. There is no gift tax at all.

You do not have to part with actual possession of a gift just because you've given it away. Indeed, there are many sophisticated maneuvers involving gifts which can lower estate taxes while at the same time allowing you to retain possession of the item given. However, this is a very tricky, often technical, area of tax law. If your estate is likely to be subject to estate tax, it's wise to talk to a lawyer who understands how to take full advantage of these rules (see Step 15).

Using Gifts To Save On Income Or Estate Taxes

Gifts can result in income tax savings if the gift is made to a person in a tax bracket lower than that of the giver.* This results because future income from the asset transferred will be taxed at lower rates each year than if the giver kept that asset and left it to the same person at death.

---

* Income over $1,000 received by children prior to their 14th birthday is taxed in their parents' bracket. After age 14, the children qualify for their own bracket, which will normally be lower than that of their parents. This means, if you plan to make gifts to your young children or grandchildren, you want to do it in a way that most income is received after age 14. EE U.S. savings bonds, which are tax-deferred until the bonds are turned in, provide one way to do this; zero-coupon tax-exempt municipal bonds are another. Ask your investment advisor for more details.

Property likely to appreciate substantially in value can also make a sensible gift. Suppose you have bought a painting or some land for $5,000, and you're confident it will increase greatly in value in a few years, to at least $50,000. If you give the painting or land away now, gift taxes will be based on the $5,000 current market value. If you wait to transfer it as part of your estate (assuming you were right about the increase in value), the painting or land would add at least $50,000 to the total of your taxable estate.

Finally, it can make excellent sense to give life insurance policies as a gift. The receiver is only taxed on the face value of the policy (assuming it's over $10,000), whereas he or she will receive a much greater amount in benefits when you die, tax free. Let's look at this in somewhat more detail.

Step 6: Understand the role of life insurance in estate planning

We have some doubts about the tendency of us Americans to over-insure our lives. Insurance company advertising that plays on our fears of disaster certainly seems shoddy. Good health seems the best life insurance we know of. Still, some life insurance can be useful, even essential. Not only can life insurance purchased at relatively low cost provide a substantial amount of money at death, but that money can usually be collected quickly. Normally, all that's needed is a certified copy of the death certificate and a completed insurance company form.

One main use of life insurance in estate planning is to provide cash for immediate needs such as family expenses or to pay your bills. If there's sufficient cash elsewhere, you don't need insurance for this purpose. However, in situations where family needs will be great, as when there are young children involved, life insurance is usually essential.

Whether life insurance proceeds are subject to federal estate taxes or not depends on who owns the policy. If the decedent owned the policy, the proceeds are included in the taxable estate. If someone else owned the policy, the proceeds are not subject to federal estate tax.* If a decedent retained any "incidents of ownership" of an insurance policy on his life, he will be held to be the owner. The "incidents of ownership" are any significant power over the insurance policy, including:

1. the right to change, or name, beneficiaries of the policy;
2. the right to borrow against the policy, or pledge any cash reserve it has, or cash it in;
3. the right to surrender, convert, or cancel the policy;
4. the right to select a payment option, e.g., the power to decide if payments to the beneficiary can be in installments rather than a lump sum;
5. the right to make payments on the policy.

---

*State laws on insurance proceeds vary; some exempt all proceeds if the decedent didn't own the policy, while others impose income taxes on recipients of proceeds above a set limit.

In many cases, there is no sound reason why the insured should retain any of the incidents of ownership of a life insurance policy. The purpose of the policy, after all, is to protect and assist someone else on the death of the insured. If there's any chance that the inclusion of the proceeds in the taxable estate will result in federal taxes being assessed, there's a strong reason to transfer ownership of the policy either by gift or by sale.

EXAMPLE: Martin, a 45-year-old family man, has an estate which includes real estate with a net worth of $350,000, stocks worth $150,000, and life insurance which will pay $300,000. His total taxable estate is worth $800,000. In other words, whenever he dies, his estate would be subject to estate tax. However, if Martin transfers ownership of his life insurance policy to someone else, such as his wife, his total estate amounts to $500,00. Thus, there will be no estate tax due, because of the estate tax credit.

If a person has what is called "an insurable interest" in another person, such as a spouse or business partner of the insured, they can take out a life insurance policy on that person. Otherwise, the insured must take out the policy, but he or she is then free to assign it (unless the policy prohibits this) to any other person. There is a risk involved in a life insurance transfer. Once you have transferred the policy, you lose your power over it forever. Suppose you assign your spouse as owner and subsequently get divorced. Do you get the policy back? No. This means you have to balance the possible death tax savings of transferring your life insurance policy with the risks inherent in loss of control.

CAUTION: For federal estate tax purposes, any transfer, by gift, of life insurance made within three years of death of the insured is disallowed, and the full amount of proceeds is included in the decedent's taxable estate. Also, gifts of life insurance made within three years of death are not entitled to the $10,000 annual gift exemption. In other words, federal law recognizes there can be substantial tax savings by excluding life insurance proceeds from the taxable estate, and prevents "last minute" transfers (within three years of death). So, when giving (transferring) life insurance, it is particularly wise to make the gift long before there appears to be any possiblity of death.

LIFE INSURANCE AND PROBATE NOTE: No matter who owns a life insurance policy, the proceeds do not have to go through probate, unless your estate is named beneficiary. Since the purpose of life insurance is to benefit other persons, it is rarely wise, or necessary, to pay the proceeds to your estate.

Step 7: Evaluate whether trusts can be used to reduce your (eventual) estate taxes

Here we enter the venerable world of trusts. The notion of a trust frightens or impresses many people. At one time, trusts were tools used to dominate industries such as oil, steel, and railroads. We also know that elaborate trusts have helped the very rich to preserve their wealth from generation to generation. Yet despite their uses to monopolize billions, trusts are quite simple in basic concept.

They work like this. The "settlor" (the person who establishes the trust) puts something of value into an entity labeled a trust. A written document called a trust instrument establishes that entity for all legal purposes. It specifies the terms under which the thing of value must be held, and distributed. It also names the "trustee," and the "beneficiary," who will benefit from the trust. Here is an example of a simple trust instrument: "I, Cynthia Senour, hereby place $20,000 in trust for my minor son, Adam Senour, until he reaches age 32 and appoint Alice Senour, my sister, as trustee of the trust."

WARNING: Though trusts are simple in concept, tax saving trusts are complicated in reality. Drafting a trust for tax savings requires the assistance of a knowledgeable lawyer. The risks of going it alone here are simply too high. See Step 15 on finding and working with a lawyer.

> *Lawful. Compatible with the will of a judge having jurisdiction.*
> — Ambrose Bierce

A tax reduction trust can be created either during your lifetime, or by your will, upon your death, in a "testamentary trust." Whenever created, a tax reduction trust must be *irrevocable* under IRS rules. Irrevocable means that once you create the trust, that's it; you cannot change or revoke it later. Legally, creating an irrevocable trust during your lifetime means you are making a gift of the property to the beneficiary(ies) and you will be assessed gift tax for any amount added to the trust which exceeds $10,000 annually.

Obviously, the fact that a trust cannot be revoked may become inconvenient if things change. On the other hand, the income tax advantage of establishing an irrevocable trust during one's life is that the income from the trust is not taxed to the person who establishes it, the settlor. The trust, or the beneficiary, will pay taxes on trust income, but that will be at a lower income bracket than the settlor's. Also, the value of the trust property is not included in the settlor's taxable estate, which can save on overall estate/gift taxes if the property appreciates in value after the trust is established.

An irrevocable life insurance trust created while you are alive can also reduce estate taxes. This is because, as we've discussed, the proceeds of a life insurance policy are considered part of the taxable estate if the decedent owned the policy at death, but permanent transference of the policy's ownership from the insured removes the proceeds from the taxable estate. One method for transferring ownership is to place the policy in a life insurance trust. As we've explained, ownership of life insurance policies can also be transferred by assigning the policy to a new owner, a much simpler method than use of a trust. So it's best not to set up a life insurance trust unless it's clear that you really need it. One situation where this sort of trust would make sense is when there is no person the policy owner trusts sufficiently to give the policy to.

EXAMPLE: Elizabeth, a single parent of a two-year-old, owns a life insurance policy for the benefit of her child. There is no adult to whom Elizabeth feels she can safely transfer ownership of the policy, so she establishes an irrevocable life insurance trust, with her daughter as beneficiary, and transfers ownership of the policy to the trust. This removes the trust proceeds from Elizabeth's taxable estate.

Finally, some trusts created by your will can save on estate taxes, though not as much as you might think. For years, the very rich could, and did, reduce the total estate taxes paid on their wealth by using trusts. One popular device was to have the bulk of a rich person's wealth left in trust for the grandchildren, while the surviving spouse and their children received the income from the trust. The wealth was subject to estate tax when the rich person died, but when the spouse died, and then when the children died, there were no additional death taxes imposed, as the wealth had never been legally owned by them, but by the trust.

Congress has passed laws curtailing these "generation-skipping transfers." Now, the full value of assets left in trust for a person's family is subject to estate tax on the death of the children. In other words, each generation is subject to a generation skipping transfer tax. Thus, if property is transferred by trust to grandchildren, tax must still be paid as if the property was first transferred to the giver's children and then by those children to the grandchildren. Similarly, this tax is now imposed on direct transfers (e.g., gifts) to a person two or more generations below the giver. However, lest you feel distressed over this added tax burden imposed on the rich, you should know the first $1,000,000 of property that skips generations is exempt from tax.* Generation-skipping trusts should be prepared by a knowledgeable lawyer. These trusts are designed to last for at least two generations, well over fifty years. There are many contingencies to consider, and many technical requirements under federal law.

Finally, perhaps the most common use of trusts is one of the simplest. This is the use of a trust to delay the age at which a minor child receives an inheritance to an age older than 18.

Many parents wish to do this, reasoning quite sensibly that if they die while their children are minors, they want some trusted adult to manage the property they leave the children, at least until those children have completed their education and are functioning in the adult world; commonly, this is an age between 25 and 30. A simple children's trust can easily be set up in your will to accomplish this purpose. This gives you the opportunity to name the trustee, establish the rules of the trust, and set the age at which any money left in the trust is turned over to your kids outright. Fortunately, establishing this sort of simple children's trust is both easy and routine. You can safely do it yourself using either *Nolo's Simple Will Book,* or our computer program, WillWriter.

NOTE ON GUARDIANSHIPS: If the parents of minor children die, the children themselves will normally be taken care of by a guardian. You should appoint such a person in your will. If you do, your choice will very likely be ratified by a court. However, relying on a guardian to manage your minor children's property may not be a wise choice, especially when a substantial amount of property is involved, because guardianships end when a child is 18, an age when many, if not most, kids do not have adequate property management abilities. For this reason, the simple children's trust is usually preferable.

Step 8: Plan to avoid probate

At this point, we enter a new phase of estate planning–the methods which can be used to avoid probate. The three major methods are joint tenancy, living trusts, and "Totten trust" bank accounts, also sometimes called "informal trusts," "savings bank trusts," and "pay on death accounts." All three methods enable you to transfer your property to inheritors without the costs and delays of probate. No one method is right for all circumstances. Often the wisest plan is to combine probate avoidance

---

* For transfers to grandchildren before 1990, the exemption is $2,000,000.

methods, for example, transferring some property by joint tenancy and other assets by living trust. Probate avoidance estate planning means determining, and then establishing, the best methods for your specific situation and needs.

JOINT TENANCY

Step 9: Understand joint tenancy as a probate avoidance technique

One of the simplest, most effective and commonly-used methods of avoiding probate is owning property in joint tenancy. For purposes of avoiding probate, the important fact about joint tenancy ownership is that it carries with it the "right of survivorship." In most states, this means that if one joint tenant dies, the other(s) automatically become the owner(s) of the whole property. Of course, death taxes must be paid on the portion owned by the decedent (if applicable), and a new deed registered. However, the property does not have to go through probate. Indeed, legally the property cannot go through probate, and you cannot will your interest in it even if you want to. The surviving joint tenant(s) get it, and that's that. By contrast, other forms of shared ownership, such as tenancy-in-common and community property do not create a right of survivorship. Each owner's share of such property can be transferred by will and can become subject to probate.

NOTE ON TENANCY-BY-THE-ENTIRETY: In a few states, the proper destination for property owned as joint tenants by married couples is tenancy-by-the-entirety. Generally speaking, the comments made here relative to joint tenancy ownership also apply to tenancy-by-the entirety.

A joint tenancy is created simply by use of the words "in joint tenancy" or "as joint tenants" when describing the property owners in the deed or other document of title. In some states it is necessary to add the words "with right of survivorship." There's no legal presumption that property is owned in joint tenancy; it must be clearly stated. It is common that land ("real property" in legalese) is owned in joint tenancy. Thus, if three people own a piece of land in joint tenancy, each owns a one-third interest in the total property. If one joint tenant dies, the others automatically get their share without probate and now own an undivided one-half interest in the property.

Any property, not just land, can be owned in joint tenancy and thereby avoid probate. It's routine to hold bank accounts, automobiles, boats, mobile homes, etc., in joint tenancy. If you don't know how you hold title to your property, be sure to find out, and consider whether you want to switch the form of ownership to joint tenancy. Before you do, though, be sure to check the law applicable to transfers of property to joint tenancy. Since there can be tax consequences, as well as technical legal requirements to follow, it's usually best to review transfers to joint tenancy with an attorney, especially if major chunks of property are involved. This sort of review should not be costly.

Joint Tenancy Safe Deposit Boxes

Safe deposit boxes can be useful items to own in joint tenancy. If the safety deposit box is jointly owned, either co-owner can obtain instant access to the documents when they are needed.

NOTE: If you want to transfer the *contents* held in a safety deposit box to the co-owner, be sure to specify on the bank documents that all property in the box is held in joint tenancy. Otherwise, the usual rule is that only the box itself, not its contents, is held in joint tenancy.

Potential Problems With Joint Tenancy

Joint tenancy can be created only by a written document (not orally) and should be used prudently, with full knowledge of its consequences. As long as both joint tenants are alive, the joint tenancy can be converted to another type of ownership by either owner whether or not the other owner consents to it, or even knows about it (this is referred to as destruction of the joint tenancy). Generally, either joint tenant has the power to sell her/his interest in the jointly-owned property at any time. The new owner takes that interest as a tenant-in-common with the original owner and there is no longer any right of survivorship. If the remaining (original) owners and the new (tenant-in-common) owners conflict, any party can seek, and obtain, a court-ordered partition into equal portions. If it isn't feasible to divide the property in this manner, the court will order a foreclosure sale with the proceeds divided accordingly.

Other problems may arise with joint tenancy, including the right of the creditors of either joint tenant to attach that tenant's interest (not all joint tenants' interests) and obtain a judicial foreclosure sale if necessary. Also, if one joint tenant becomes incompetent or senile, this can render it difficult and time-consuming for the other owners to manage the property. So joint tenancy should be used only with someone you completely trust. In many family situations, where this trust exists, joint tenancy is the best way to avoid probate, because it is so simple.

Joint tenancy does not reduce the death taxes. It is solely a probate avoidance device. Both state and federal governments include the value of a decedent's share of jointly owned property in his or her taxable estate. The amount of that interest is based on the decedent's financial contribution to the purchase of the joint property. Thus, if the decedent had put up all the money to purchase an item of joint property, the full market value of that property would be included in his or her taxable estate. This means that if you and your sister set up a joint tenancy in a piece of land and you paid for it, the full value of that land will be included in your taxable estate. However, if you paid a gift tax earlier for the one-half interest you gave to your sister, or if it was transferred for value, such as in exchange for your sister taking care of your children each summer for ten years, only your half would be included.

Moreover, except for husband and wife joint tenancies, the tax authorities will presume that the first joint tenant to die contributed *all* the cash for the purchase (and maintenance, if additional money was required for that) of jointly owned property.

The burden of proof is on the surviving tenant(s) to overturn this presumption by establishing that the survivors made cash or other contributions toward the purchase or upkeep of the jointly owned property or received it as a gift. To the extent the surviving tenants can show contribution, the taxable estate will be reduced proportionately. Thus, one risk with holding property in joint tenancy is that if the owners keep poor records, the property may be subjected to death taxes twice.

Community Property, Basis and Title to Property

Residents of states with community property owner laws (California, Idaho, Washington, Nevada, Arixona, Texas, New Mexico and Wisconsin*) may prefer to hold title to marital property as "community property" or "as community property in joint tenancy." To understand why, you have to know how the federal tax "basis" laws work. Simply put, the "basis" given to property is the value put upon it to determine the subsequent profit (or loss) when it is sold. For example, if you buy a chair for $50 and sell it a year later for $200, your tax basis is $50 and your taxable profit is $150.

Normally, the basis of property is its acquisition cost, plus the cost of any improvements. However, when a person dies, federal tax law states that the "basis" of property received by inheritors is "stepped-up" to its value at the date of the original owner's death. Thus, to continue the previous exmple, if you left the chair by will to your nephew Frank and the chair is worth $200 on the date of your death, Frank's basis in the chair becomes $200 (not $50).

The desirability of owning property as community property in those states where this is possible is traceable to one additional tax basis rule. In a community property state, at the death of one spouse, both halves of the community property are automatically entitled to a stepped-up tax basis. To put this another way, not only is the half of the property owned by the deceased spouse entitled to a stepped up basis, so, too, is the half of the property owned by the surviving spouse. What this means is explained in the following example.

EXAMPLE: Suppose Alicia and Harold have been married for 30 years. During that time they've acquired the following valuable community property:**

• a home, purchased for $30,000 in 1955, worth $300,000 in 1988;

• a summer home, purchased for $50,000 in 1964, worth $200,000 in 1988;

• two oil paintings, purchased for $3,000 each in 1960, worth $100,000 cash in 1988.

Harold dies in 1988. He leaves his half of the community property he owns with Alicia to their children. This means they receive $150,000 worth of the home, $100,000 worth of the summer home, and a painting worth $100,000.

Alicia, of course, owns property of the same value because it represents her one-half of the community property. All of this property, i.e., both the half received by the children and the half that Alicia obtains as her share of the former community property, is entitled to a stepped-up basis. In other words, if Alicia decided to sell her oil painting for $100,000 a week after her husband's death, she would owe no tax. Similarly, if Alicia and the children decided to sell the summer home for $200,000, no tax would be owned by anyone. Which brings us back to the point we started with: community property ownership can be a superior way to own property than is joint tenancy ownership.

The problem is that the IRS presumes that joint tenancy property is NOT community property, which means that both halves are not entitled to a stepped up tax

---

* Community property is owned one-half by each spouse with each being free to dispose of their one-half at death by a will or other estate planning device.

** Community property is owned one-half by each spouse with each being free to dispose of their one-half at death by a will or other estate planning device.

basis. This is not the same thing as saying that joint tenancy property cannot be entitled to a stepped up basis for both halves of the property. In fact, if community property is held in joint tenancy, BOTH halves of that property are entitled to a stepped up basis upon the death of a spouse if the community property status can be proved.

Unfortunately, this can often present a problem, as IRS rules are far from clear concerning what proof suffices to establish the community property status.

As a result, many estate planners generally advise married couples in community property states not to hold property, especially appreciated property, in joint tenancy to be sure they obtain a stepped up basis for both halves of their property. A problem with this approach, however, is that property held as community property has to be probated in some states, even if left to a surviving spouse. To avoid probate and qualify for a stepped up tax basis, your best bet may be to hold title to your property as "community property held in joint tenancy."

Step 10: Understand revocable trusts as a probate avoidance technique

Living Trusts

As we saw earlier, trusts can be relatively simple devices in theory. Probate avoidance trusts, called "living" or "intervivos" (Latin for "among the living") trusts, can be simple in practice. Moreover, a living trust can be, and generally is, revocable. In other words, you don't have to make an irrevocable transfer of property to a living trust to obtain the benefit of avoiding probate.

Here's how you set up a living trust. First, you create a trust document and then transfer property into the trust. This can be cash, tangible objects such as heirlooms, jewelry, real estate, or any asset of value. The trust becomes the legal owner of that property. You name yourself as trustee with full power to control and manage the trust property while you live. You specify the beneficiary, or beneficiaries, who will receive the trust property when you die. You also name a successor trustee to distribute the property to those beneficiaries after your death. You retain the power to revoke or change the trust whenever you want to. Upon your death, the property in the trust is transferred probate-free to the beneficiary(ies). Living trusts thus transfer property outside of probate without the risks associated with joint tenancy. With a living trust, there's no danger that the person you ultimately want to receive your property can exercise premature ownership rights.

A basic living trust can be a three- or four-page document. Of course, like any trust, living trusts can become far more complicated. You can adopt complex administrative or distributive provisions, particularly if you don't want all the property transferred outright to the beneficiaries immediately after your death. If you find a suitable research source, you can prepare a simple probate avoidance living trust yourself. Do be sure you've checked your state's laws, because the laws applicable to living trusts vary somewhat. For instance, a minority of states require notice to be given to beneficiaries if a living trust has been revoked, or if they have been removed as beneficiaries, while most states do not.*

Aside from the initial work of drafting a living trust, there is little other red tape involved. Normally a living trust does not have to be filed with any official agency, or recorded. If you (the settlor) make yourself the trustee, as is the usual case, all trust

---

*PLAN YOUR ESTATE: WILLS, PROBATE AVOIDANCE, TRUSTS & TAXES by Denis Clifford is published in both a California and Texas edition by Nolo Press. Both contain an intervivos trust form and instructions on how to prepare it.

income transactions can be reported on your income tax return and no separate income tax returns have to be filed for the trust. However, some paperwork is usually involved in establishing the trust. Title to property transferred to the trust must be actually put into the trust's name. Thus, ownership of stock must be re-registered and new certificates issued, and real estate deeds must be prepared listing the trust as owner of real property, and then recorded. Usually the hassle of this paperwork is small when balanced against the savings to the estate achieved by avoiding probate.

Totten Trusts — A Special Type Of Bank Account

"Totten" trusts (named for Mr. Totten, who established the trust's validity) are a simple means of retaining control over bank deposits while you live and yet passing them to your inheritors free of probate upon your death. This device is also sometimes called a "savings bank" trust, an "informal trust" or a "pay on death account." Here's how it works. You simply open a bank account–usually a savings account–in your name as depositor, as trustee for the benefit of whomever you choose. For example, if Ray Jones wants to leave cash, probate-free, to his daughter, he opens a Totten trust account as "Ray Jones, depositor, as trustee for Michele Jones, beneficiary." Banks have standard forms for opening a Totten trust account. No other forms or legalities are required, and a Totten trust account is not more trouble than a regular savings account. Banks do not normally charge extra fees for holding money in Totten trust accounts.

Totten trusts have certain benefits not enjoyed by joint tenancy accounts. Principal among these is that the beneficiary has absolutely no right to any money while the depositor is alive. The depositor can also close the account whenever he likes, and can change the beneficiary at any time. Also he can withdraw, or deposit, any amount desired. Because the depositor retains complete control over the account until death, the establishment of a Totten trust is not a gift, and so is not subject to gift tax. However, the beneficiary of a Totten trust is liable for a pro rata share of any death taxes assessed against the depositor's estate, as any amounts in Totten trusts are included in the taxable estate.

After the depositor's death, all that is necessary for the beneficiary to obtain the money is the bank account book, personal identification, a certified copy of the death certificate, and release from death tax liens, if there are any. In other words, the money can usually be transferred free of probate costs within a few days of death.

Step 11: Understand the other uses of trusts

Trusts can serve important practical estate planning needs beyond probate avoidance or tax reduction. A major use of trusts is to impose controls over property left to inheritors. The use of a trust to leave property to your children was discussed in Step 7. Aside from these types of simple children's trusts, a trust for control purposes usually requires the assistance of a knowledgeable lawyer, as the risk of going it completely alone are, we fear, substantial. The best we can do here is to give you a brief overview of some of the considerations involved.

It is possible to control what an inheritor can do with the property left to them in a number of ways by inserting specific language in the trust document. People who feel the need to put conditions on the money or property they leave usually do so for one of the following reasons:

• Trusts for charitable purposes: You want the income from a sum of money put in trust used over a period of years to further certain social or charitable goals.

• The beneficiary is incompetent: When a beneficiary is incompetent, the law requires supervision of assets left to him or her. Establishing a trust normally provides a much better method of control than using a court-supervised guardian or conservator because a trust can be geared to the specifics of the particular situation. Also, trustees are usually able to legally exercise more flexibility and creativity than guardians or custodians, since they do not normally need court approval for trust management decisions, as guardians or custodians often do.

• The beneficiary may be irresponsible: Occasionally, people want to give money or other property to benefit someone, but want controls imposed because they are worried the beneficiary is unable to manage money, and they want to prevent him from squandering his inheritance. The actual term for this is a "spendthrift trust."

• The first beneficiary is only to get the interest (not principal): It is common for a person making an estate plan to want a particular beneficiary to receive the income generated by a sum of money during his lifetime. After that, the lump sum used to generate the interest is to go to someone else. For example, Jane might want her spouse Jim to get the interest income from $250,000 while he lives, with the principal to be divided between Jane's children from her first marriage, when he dies. This type of trust is commonly called a "life estate trust" because the property left in the trust for the use of the first beneficiary for his or her life (called the "life beneficiary") passes to other beneficiaries when the life beneficiary dies. The advantage of this type of trust is that the original property owner is able to control who gets the property after the life beneficiary dies.

The usual way to create a life estate is by a trust. Drafting this type of trust requires the assistance of a lawyer. It may seem simple at first, but it is not. For example, here are only a few of the questions that can arise:

• Does the surviving spouse, the one with the "life estate" interest, have the right to sell the trust property?

• Suppose the surviving spouse has massive medical bills? Can he encumber the trust property to get money to pay the bills?

• What rights do the final beneficiaries have to learn what the life beneficiary is doing with the property?

All these problems and more should be resolved in the language establishing the trust. There are also technical IRS requirements which must be met, and a mistake in complying with these can be disastrous in tax terms. Furthermore, since a trust cannot be changed or amended once the will writer dies and may last for many years, a poorly drafted trust can cause all sorts of problems down the road.

Step 12: Understand wills

I have nothing
I owe a great deal
The rest I leave to the poor.
— Complete will of 15th Century
French author Rabelais

Wills can be formidable documents. Many people are reluctant to prepare one because they worry they'll become enmeshed in legal complexities. Sometimes lurking behind this reluctance is the superstition that thinking about a will, or preparing one, might somehow hasten death. Fortunately, preparing a will doesn't have to be a horrendous, or expensive, procedure. After all, a will is basically a document setting forth your directions about what happens to your property after your death. As we've discussed, transferring property by will incurs the major drawback of probate. We've urged you to avoid probate and discussed the primary methods of doing that. Does this mean you shouldn't prepare a will at all? No. In most cases, it's wise to have a will for at least one of the following reasons.

• Wills can be useful to pass small amounts of personal property (the antique coffee pot to Aunt Lucy, the baseball card collection to Cousin Martin, etc.) without the bother of creating trusts or joint tenancies. This sort of will often does not have to be probated, as many states exempt wills which leave small amounts from probate. For example, in California, wills which transfer less than $60,000 (and no real estate) do not require probate.

• You might receive money unexpectedly from a surprise gift or bequest, the Irish sweepstakes, a forgotten lawsuit, etc., so it's sensible to have a "catch-all" will covering this contingency. State law would otherwise determine who receives this property and those laws are inflexible and rarely distribute property as you would choose.

• A will is a good place to prepare for the remote but tragic possibility that you and your spouse should die in a common disaster. It can prevent double taxation as well as arrange for eventual property distribution.

• Wills provide a means for you to name guardians of your childrens' property (especially any you leave to them) and to suggest a guardian of minor children themselves. You cannot will your children—they are obviously not property. This means you can't insure that someone you don't want to gain custody (an ex-spouse, for instance) will be denied it. However, a statement in a will of why you believe your suggested guardian should have custody may be persuasive to a court. This is especially true if the other parent is dead, has abandoned the children, or is legally incompetent.

• A will affords you the opportunity to name your executor, the person with legal authority to handle problems regarding your estate which you may not have anticipated.

COMMON SENSE NOTE: Don't develop an irrational fear of wills and probate. Assuming that much, if not most, of your property is transferred outside of probate, the fees for probating your will should be minimal. Probate fees are generally based on the value (market value, not equity) of your probate estate. Also, most probate avoidance techniques, such as living trusts, are more trouble to maintain than in a will. For this reason, many younger people who prefer to prepare a will now and leave more sophisticated estate planning for later.

Okay, let's say we've convinced you a will is a good idea. How do you go about preparing one? Most people can safely prepare their own wills by using form books prepared for the nonlawyer. The best of these (we say modestly) is *The Simple Will Book* by Denis Clifford (Nolo Press). In addition, Nolo publishes WillWriter, a computer program which will help you prepare your own will using an Apple II, Macintosh, IBM P.C., I.B.M. P.C.-compatible or Commodore 64 computer.

Also, you can, of course, hire a lawyer. In that case it's wise to define your basic goals before you talk to the lawyer. You should only be hiring the lawyer to handle the technical aspect of will drafting, not to make dcisions for you. See our discussion in Step 14 on how to find and deal with lawyers.

The legal requirements of a formal will are probably fewer than you would expect. They include the following:

• The will must be typed, or printed. Some states permit hand written wills or "holographic" wills, but most don't. In any case, we don't recommend them, except in emergencies or as a stop-gap measure until a formal will can be prepared.

• The document must state that it is your will. No specific substantive provisions are required. Normally, you will want to specify your executor and state that "no bond is required."

• You must sign and date it.

• It must be signed, and dated by three witnesses (some states only require two witnesses). The witnesses should be "disinterested," i.e., get nothing from your will.

You can do almost anything you want in a will except leave property for illegal purposes, and, in some states, disinherit your spouse and/or children.* Otherwise, there is almost no limit on what you can do, or say. Once your will is prepared, leave it in a safe place, and be sure someone, at least your executor, knows it's location.

> *Gouveneur Morris, revolutionary war statesman,*
> *married late in life to young Ann Randolph.*
> *When he died in 1816, he left her a substantial*
> *income from his estate with the provision that*
> *if she married again . . . the income doubled.*

---

*In some states, you cannot disinherit your wife or children; they have a right to a certain minimum percentage of your estate. In some other states, you can only disinherit your wife or children by specifically stating that you are doing so. If you simply fail to mention them, they will inherit anyway. See a lawyer if this concerns you.

Step 13: Decide whether you wish to make a will

Although this book does not enable you to draft your own will, we do provide you a framework for focusing on whether you want one.

If you do want to make a will, we have prepared the following worksheet. This allows you to sort out which property is to be left to which inheritor. We also provide room for you to put the estimated value of the property. This will help you to check whether your estate might be worth enough to warrant estate tax planning, in the event you have skipped earlier sections of this part. In addition, because you may wish to leave certain items to certain people on a conditional basis only (e.g., "I leave my camera equipment to my nephew David if he has graduated from college prior to my death, otherwise to my niece Joanna"), the worksheet has room for you to make such specifications. Once that is done, you can visit a lawyer and have your actual will drafted (or use a self-help resource if one is available for your state) for a moderate fee.

Payment of Debts

Finally, we have reserved space for you to indicate your desires regarding the payment of debts which may exist upon your death. This is very important. Your will is a place where you can designate how your debts are to be paid. If you make no provision for this, your estate will pay your debts on a pro rata basis from the property left to all your inheritors. This can have disastrous consequences for those heirs who receive tangible property, such as heirlooms, but no cash. In such a case, the heirloom might have to be sold to meet the heir's pro rata tax obligation.

will of the wisp

Item of property	Inheritor	Estimated Net Value	Conditions	Payment of Debts

193

If there is no formal probate, or only a nominal amount of money is transferred through the probate system, how will your debts get paid? Good question. A decedent's assets remain liable for debts even after they're transferred. If you have only one inheritor, that person will be responsible for paying your debts from your inherited property. If there are several inheritors, the responsibility for paying the debts can be hard to determine. Thus, you should definitely arrange payment of your debts by some certain methods, to reduce the chance of lawsuits by creditors or confusion among inheritors. Start, of course, by adding up the total amount of your debts, referring to the list you wrote in Part I. Then allocate specific assets to pay them.

If you do not take care of this question in your will, make sure and tell whoever will be responsible for distributing your estate what your plan for debt payment is. Finally, write that plan down. Often it can be included as part of a living trust.

Step 14: Consider the choices for the disposition of your body

Funeral. A pageant whereby we attest to our respect to the dead by enriching the undertaker, and strengthen our grief by an expenditure that deepens our groans and doubles our tears.

— Ambrose Bierce

It's often awkward to think, or talk, about the reality of body disposition. Many people also find it difficult to plan for that reality. Commonly, if no planning is done, family or friends will turn uncritically to "professionals," usually funeral parlors. Sometimes this is done without reflection or knowledge of what alternatives actually exist.

Part of thorough etate planning is determining what arrangement you want for disposition of your body. Among the choices are a "traditional" funeral, complete with embalming and open-casket viewing; an inexpensive funeral through membership in a funeral society; cremation; donation of your body to a medical school or other research institution; and donation of body parts for transplants (areas of great need include kidneys, corneas and hearts). It's also important to arrange for a burial plot or the distribution of your ashes. If you're concerned, we suggest you:

• Contact the nearest non-profit funeral society to see what they offer.

• Plan whatever ceremony you deem suitable and pay for it in advance or make sure appropriate funds are made available and designated.

• Leave a letter of instructions in a place where it will be available upon your death. You can include these instructions in your will.

• Make appropriate agreements for body part donations, and for termination of life support when it only prolongs the moment of death. A sample "living will" for this is included here. A more comprehensive and legally secure method for terminating life support systems is to prepare a durable power of attorney. Forms for this are found in *The Power of Attorney Book*, Nolo Press.

A Living Will

TO MY FAMILY, MY PHYSICIAN, MY LAWYER, MY CLERGYMAN

TO ANY MEDICAL FACILITY IN WHOSE CARE I HAPPEN TO BE

TO ANY INDIVIDUAL WHO MAY BECOME RESPONSIBLE FOR MY HEALTH, WELFARE
    OR AFFAIRS:

Death is as much a reality as birth, growth, maturity and old age — it is the one certainty of life. If the time comes when I, _____, can no longer take part in decisions for my own future, let this statement stand as an expression of my wishes while I am still of sound mind.

If the situation should arise in which there is no reasonable expectation of my recovery from physical or mental disability, I request that I be allowed to die and not be kept alive by artificial means or "heroic measures." I do not fear death itself as much as the indignities of deterioration, dependence and hopeless pain. I, therefore, ask that medication be mercifully administered to me to alleviate suffering even though this may hasten the moment of death.

This request is made after careful consideration. I hope you who care for me will feel morally bound to follow its mandate. I recognize that this appears to place a heavy responsibility upon you, but it is with the intention of relieving you of such responsibility and of placing it upon myself in accordance with my strong convictions, that this statement is made.

Signed _____

Date: _____

Witness: _____

Witness: _____
Copies of this request have been given to:

_____

_____

_____

Step 15: Decide if you need a lawyer

Lawyer: one skilled in circumvention of the law.
— Ambrose Bierce

Unless you have an estate larger than $600,000 or fairly complicated desires, you can do most of the necessary planning work yourself. Of course, you may want to check your work with a knowledgeable lawyer, or you may be a person who simply doesn't want to learn the "ins and outs" of making a simple will, or living trust, and wants to hire a lawyer to do it for you.

Hiring a competent lawyer who will charge a reasonable fee isn't always easy. Ask any lawyer you approach specific questions about your concerns. Do you get clear, concise answers? If not, try someone else. If the lawyer acts wise, but says little except to ask that the problem be placed in his hands (with a substantial fee, of course) watch out! You are either talking with someone who doesn't know the answer and won't admit it (common) or someone who finds it impossible to let go of the "me expert, you plebeian" philosophy (even more common). It should go without saying that you don't want to be a passive client* or deal with a lawyer who wants you to play that role.

If you have no contacts with lawyers and don't know where to turn, here are some suggestions:

• Be wary of referral panels set up by local bar associations. Normally, any local lawyer can get on these panels by paying a fee. Although there are many good lawyers who list on these panels, they also attract more than a few whose main reason for being there is a shortage of clients.

• Check with a local consumer organization to see if they can recommend someone;

• Talk to friends or associates who have small business experience. These people will almost always have a continuing relationship with a lawyer. If their attorney doesn't do estate work, they should at least be able to supply you with a good referral.

---

*The Latin root word "client" is "to hear," "to obey."

Even if you have done most of the initial estate planning work yourself, a consultation with a lawyer is often a sensible step. A knowledgeable lawyer can review your work and/or help you put it into final form. They can also insure your estate plan complies with all your state's legal requirements, and remove any anxieties you might feel if you attempt to do all the work yourself. If you do a good deal of the initial work yourself, the lawyer's fee should not be large. We recommend you discuss all potential fees in detail before you turn your estate planning over to any lawyer.

Step 16: Help yourself by researching the law of your state

Lawyers are experts at recycling information and charging healthy amounts for this rather limited service. We say limited because when faced with a particular legal task, lawyers (or their paralegal assistants or secretaries) often do little more than open a book of legal forms and copy out already prepared material. For example, many routine wills are taken directly from standard legal form books and then the few blanks filled in. Even in more complicated situations of estate planning, lawyers often do little more than look up the answer in one of the established texts or encyclopedias on the subject. Why can't you do this for yourself?

Often you can if you know where to look. Unfortunately, state laws on estate matters vary significantly. This means if you wish to plan your own estate with no attorney help, you will have to do some legal research unless you live in California or Texas.* Start at your local law library. These are usually supported by your tax dollars, or the fees you pay to file legal papers, and are open to the public. There is usually one in your principal county courthouse. The best research tools are often how-to-do-it books written primarily for lawyers. The best book explaining how to use legal libraries, and do your own research is *Legal Research: How to Find and Understand the Law* by Stephen Elias (Nolo Press).

NOTE: An alternative to spending time in the law library is to create your own general estate plan and then check it with a local lawyer to be sure it meets the technical requirements of your state.

D. Wrap Up

There are many choices to consider as part of creating a good estate plan. Understanding these choices can take some time. The real question is whether you consider it worth your effort to learn how to maximize the money you can leave to your inheritors, and minimize the money consumed by lawyers and taxes. Since modest effort can result in substantial savings, we suggest that you do prepare a careful estate plan, getting suitable professional help when you need it.

---

*Most books on estate planning written specifically for the lay person contain general advice and are not geared to each state's laws. There are at least two exceptions, however. *Plan Your Estate: Wills, Probate Avoidance, Trusts & Taxes* is published in two state editions: Texas and California (see back of this book for more information). These books contain all the information the average resident of these states will need to competently plan a small or moderate-sized estate.

PART IV

Continuations

About the Authors

Denis Clifford is an expert in the fields of probate avoidance and estate planning. He is the author of the best selling book, *Plan Your Estate: Wills, Probate Avoidance, Trusts & Taxes* (California and Texas editions). Denis is the eldest of seven children of an Irish-American family. He happily attends his family's yearly summer reunion and is interested in family lore. A graduate of Columbia Law School, where he was an editor of the law review, Denis practiced law for a number of years before changing his career to write self-help law books for Nolo Press.

Carol Pladsen has studied the field of family history for many years. She began with a search for her own Norwegian roots and then became interested in the process by which other families stay in contact and record their histories. She has organized successful family reunions and developed a number of other techniques to help families communicate. Although born and raised in Minnesota she is now delighted to call California her home. She is the associate publisher of Nolo Press.

About the Illustrator

Mari Stein is a free lance illustrator and writer. Her published work has been eclectic, covering a wide range of subjects: humor, whimsy, health education, juvenile, fables and yoga. Among the books she has written and illustrated are *Some Thoughts for My Friends,* and *VD The Love Epidemic.* She has also illustrated childrens' books, textbooks, magazine articles, and a book of poetry. For Nolo Press she has illustrated *29 Reasons Not to Go to Law School, Author Law,* and *Media Law.* She works out of a studio in her Pacific Palisades home, where she lives with her rabbits, cultivates roses, and teaches yoga.

UPDATE SERVICE
• Introductory Offer •

Our books are as current as we can make them, but sometimes the laws do change between editions. You can read about law changes which may affect this book in the NOLO NEWS, a 16-page newspaper which we publish quarterly.

In addition to the Update Service, each issue contains comprehensive articles about the growing self-help law movement as well as areas of law that are sure to affect you. (regular subscription rate is $7.00)

To receive the next 4 issues of the NOLO NEWS, please send us $2.00:

Name _____

Address _____

_____

Send to: NOLO PRESS, 950 Parker St., Berkeley CA 94710

Recycle Your Out-of-Date Books & Get 30% off your next purchase!

Using an old edition can be dangerous if information in it is wrong. Unfortunately, laws and legal procedures change often. To help you keep up to date we extend this offer. If you cut out and deliver to us the title portion of the cover of any old Nolo book we'll give you a 30% discount off the retail price of any new Nolo book. For example, if you have a copy of TENANT'S RIGHTS, 4th edition and want to trade it for the latest CALIFORNIA MARRIAGE AND DIVORCE LAW, send us the TENANT'S RIGHTS cover and a check for the current price of MARRIAGE & DIVORCE, less a 30% discount. Information on current prices and editions is listed in the NOLO NEWS (see above box). Generally speaking, any book more than two years old is of questionable value. Books more than four or five years old are a menace.

OUT OF DATE = DANGEROUS

This offer is to individuals only.

How To Form Your Own Corporation
All the forms, Bylaws, Articles, stock certificates and instructions necessary to file your small profit corporation in California.

California Edition	$24.95
Texas Edition	$21.95
New York Edition	$19.95
Florida Edition	$19.95

The Non-Profit Corporation Handbook
Includes all the forms, Bylaws, Articles and instructions you need to form a non-profit corporation in California.

California Only $24.95

Bankruptcy: Do It Yourself
Step-by-step instructions and all the forms you need.

National Edition $14.95

Legal Care For Your Software
Protect your software through the use of trade secret, trademark, copyright, patents, contracts and agreements.

National Edition $24.95

The Dictionary of Intellectual Property Law
Provides functional and contextual definitions for the hundreds of law-related terms commonly used in high technology computer commerce.

National Edition $17.95

The Partnership Book
A basic primer for people who are starting a small business together. Sample agreements, buy-out clauses, limited partnerships.

National Edition $17.95

Plan Your Estate: Wills, Probate Avoidance, Trusts and Taxes
Making a will, alternatives to probate, living trusts, limiting inheritance and estate taxes, and more.

California Edition $15.95

WillWriter - a software/book package
Use your computer to prepare and update your own valid will. Runs on Apple II+, IIe, IIc, the Mac, the IBM PC (and most PC compatibles).

National Edition $49.95

Nolo's Simple Will Book
Shows you how to draft a will without a lawyer in any state except Louisiana.

National Edition $14.95

The Power of Attorney Book
Covers the process which allows you to arrange for someone else to protect your rights and property should you become incapable of doing so.

National Edition $14.95

Chapter 13: The Federal Plan to Repay Your Debts
The alternative to straight bankruptcy. This book helps you develop a plan to pay your debts over a three year period. All forms and worksheets included.

National Edition $14.95

Billpayers' Rights
Bankruptcy, student loans, bill collectors and collection agencies, credit cards, car repossessions, child support, etc.

California only $12.95

The California Professional Corporation Handbook
All the forms and instructions to form a professional corporation.

California only $29.95

Small Time Operator
How to start and operate your own small business, keep books and pay taxes.

National Edition $9.95

How to Settle a Simple Estate
Forms and instructions necessary to wind up a California resident's estate after death.

California Edition $19.95

How to Do Your Own Divorce
All the forms for an uncontested dissolution. Instructions included.

California Edition	$12.95
Texas Edition	$12.95

California Marriage and Divorce Law
Community and separate property, debts, children, buying a house, etc. Sample pre-nuptial contracts, simple will, probate avoidance information.

California only $14.95

How to Modify & Collect Child Support in Calif.
How to change and enforce child support payments. Complete with forms and instructions.

California only $17.95

The Living Together Kit
Legal guide for unmarried couples. Covers wills, living together contracts, children, medical emergencies, etc.

National Edition $14.95

Sourcebook For Older Americans
Most comprehensive resource tool on income, rights and benefits of Americans over 55. Social security, Medicare, pensions, etc.

National Edition $14.95

How to Adopt Your Stepchild
How to prepare all forms and appear in court.

California only $17.95

A Legal Guide for Lesbian/Gay Couples
Raising children, buying property, wills, job discrimination and more.

National Edition $17.95

Start Up Money: How to Finance Your New Small Business
How to write a business plan, obtain a loan package and find sources of finance.

National Edition $12.95

Patent It Yourself
Complete instructions on how to do a patent search and file a patent in the U.S.

National Edition $24.95

How to Copyright Software
Covers common mistakes and how to correct them, failure to register, problems with protection and the Computer Copyright Act.

National Edition $24.95

The People's Law Review
50-state catalog of self-help law materials, articles and interviews.

National Edition $8.95

Fight Your Ticket
Preparing for court, arguing your case, cross-examining witnesses, etc.

California only $12.95

Legal Research: How to Find and Understand the Law
Comprehensive guide to doing your own legal research.

National Edition $14.95

Tenants' Rights
Everything tenants need to know to protect themselves.

California Edition $14.95

Everybody's Guide to Small Claims Court
Step-by-step guide to going to small claims court and collecting a judgment.

California Edition	$10.95
National Edition	$10.95

How to Change Your Name
All the forms and instructions you need.
California only $14.95

Homestead Your House
All the forms and instructions you need.
California only $8.95

Author Law
Publishing contracts, copyright, royalties, libel and invasion of privacy. Includes index and glossary.
National Edition $14.95

The Criminal Records Book
Takes you through all the procedures available to get your records sealed, destroyed or changed. Forms and instructions.
California only $14.95

The Landlord's Law Book: Rights and Responsibilities
Covers discrimination, insurance, tenants' privacy, leases, security deposits, rent control, liability and rent withholding.
California only $19.95

The Landlord's Law Book: Evictions
All the forms and instructions you need to evict a tenant.
California Edition $19.95

The Independent Paralegal's Handbook: How to Provide Legal Services Without Going to Jail
How to open legal typing office to provide paralegal services
National Edition $12.95

California Civil Code
(West Publishing) Statutes covering a wide variety of topics.
California only $16.50

California Code of Civil Procedure
(West Publishing) Statutes governing most judicial and administrative procedures.
California only $16.50

Landlording
Maintenance and repairs, getting good tenants, avoiding evictions, taxes, etc.
National Edition $17.95

Your Family Records: How to Preserve Personal, Financial and Legal History
Probate avoidance, organizing records and documents, genealogical research. For existing and future family generations.
National Edition $14.95

Marketing Without Advertising
A creative and practical guide that shows small businesspersons how to avoid wasting money on advertising. The authors, experienced business consultants, show how to implement an ongoing marketing plan to tell potential and current customers that yours is a quality business worth trusting, recommending and coming back to.
National Edition $14.00

Make Your Own Contract
Tear-out contracts for lending money, selling personal property, leasing personal proeprty, storing valuables, etc.
National Edition $12.95

Media Law: A Legal Handbook for the Working Journalist
Censorship, libel and invasion of privacy. Newsroom searches, access to news sources, reporter's privilege and more.
National Edition $14.95

How to Become A United States Citizen
Explains the naturalization process from filing to the oath of allegiance. Text is in both English and Spanish.
National Edition $9.95

All About Escrow
Gives you a good understanding of what your escrow officer should be doing for you.
National Edition $10.95

Annulment: Your Chance to Remarry Within the Catholic Church Explains procedures by which Roman Catholics can obtain annulments.
National Edition $5.95

The Buyer's Guide: Inspecting a Home or Income Property
A realistic and practical approach to inspecting residential and income property.
National Edition $15.95

Homebuyers: Lambs to the Slaughter
Describes how sellers, agents, lenders & lawyers are out to fleece the buyer & how to protect yourself.
National Edition $12.95

29 Reasons Not to Go to Law School
A humorous and irreverent look at the dubious pleasures of going to law school. $6.95

---

self-help law books

Order Form

Qty. Title   Unit   Total

Prices subject to change

Tax: (CA only; San Mateo, LA, Santa Clara & Bart Counties, 6 1/2%, all others, 6%

name_____

address_____

_____

____Visa ____Mastercard

#_____ exp._____

signature_____

phone (   )_____

subtotal _____
tax _____
postage & handling _____
Total _____

Credit card information or a check may be sent to NOLO Press, 950 Parker St., Berkeley CA 94710 or call (415) 549-1976
or
Send a check only to NOLO Distributing, Box 544, Occidental CA 95465

Plan Your Estate:
WILLS, PROBATE AVOIDANCE, TRUSTS & TAXES

By Attorney Denis Clifford

Like the other do-it-yourself manuals from Nolo Press, Plan Your Estate *is particularly helpful to the layperson who does not want to consult a lawyer . . . a clear, comprehensive and even charming book, focused specifically on California law and tax regulations.*
Los Angeles Times

Plan Your Estate provides comprehensive information on making a will, alternatives to probate, planning to limit inheritance and estate taxes, living trusts and providing for family and friends. An explanation of the new statutory will and tear-out forms are included.

SIMPLE WILL BOOK

by Attorney Denis Clifford

This book will show you how to draft a will without a lawyer in any state except Louisiana. Covers all the basics, including what to do about children, whom you can designate to carry out your wishes, and how to comply with the technical legal requirements of each state. Includes examples and many alternative clauses.

YOUR FAMILY RECORDS: How to Preserve Personal, Financial and Legal History

Here is the special offer we mentioned in the introduction. Send us this coupon and get a second book for $5.95 (plus tax & postage). You must send us this coupon, not a copy.

Everyone should buy this book.

Tom Vacar,
Lawyer and consumer columnist

YOUR FAMILY RECORDS	$5.95
+ tax (CA only)	
+ postage	1.00
TOTAL ENCLOSED	_____

Name _____

Address _____

City _____ State _____ Zip _____

■ SEND TO: NOLO PRESS, 950 Parker Street, Berkeley, CA 94710 ■